Creating Art Quilts with Panels

Easy Thread Painting and Embellishing Techniques to Create Your Own Colorful Piece of Art from Panels

Joyce Hughes

Landauer Publishing

Dedication

To Kyle, thank you for believing in me and seeing my talents before I saw them for myself. You encouraged me to show people my quilts, and now people can see them and make their own quilts through this book. Your loving soul will continue to grow . . .

Creating Art Quilts with Panels

Landauer Publishing is an imprint of Fox Chapel Publishing Company, Inc.

Copyright © 2019 by Joyce Hughes and Fox Chapel Publishing Company, Inc., 903 Square Street, Mount Joy, PA 17552.

Vice President–Content: Christopher Reggio; Editor: Colleen Dorsey; Copy Editor: Anthony Regolino; Designer: Wendy Reynolds; Photographers: Joyce Hughes and Sue Voegtlin; Indexer: Jay Kreider

Images of complete panels on pages 7, 8, 9, 10 (left and bottom), and 11 (left and middle) graciously provided with permission by Northcott Silk Inc.

Shutterstock photos: page 13 (bottom left): haris M; pages 43 (bottom), 127: okskaz; page 65 (bottom right): BERMIX STUDIO; page 68 (bottom left): Garsya; page 68 (bottom right): wasanajai

ISBN 978-1-947163-16-4

Library of Congress Cataloging-in-Publication Data

Names: Hughes, Joyce, 1961- author.
Title: Creating art quilts with panels / Joyce Hughes.
Description: Mount Joy, PA : Landauer Publishing is an imprint of Fox Chapel Publishing Company, Inc., [2019] | Includes index.
Identifiers: LCCN 2018038110 (print) | LCCN 2018038695 (ebook) | ISBN 9781607656890 () | ISBN 9781947163164 (softcover)
Subjects: LCSH: Quilting–Patterns. | Appliqué–Patterns. | Art quilts.
Classification: LCC TT835 (ebook) | LCC TT835 .H815 2019 (print) | DDC 746.46/041–dc23
LC record available at https://lccn.loc.gov/2018038110

We are always looking for talented authors. To submit an idea, please send a brief inquiry to acquisitions@foxchapelpublishing.com.

Printed in China
22 21 20 19   2 4 6 8 10 9 7 5 3

Contents

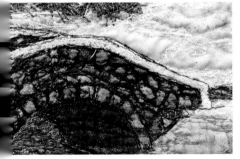

Acknowledgments

Thanks to:

My husband, John, my daughter, Emily, and my mom: Your encouragement and support have made me the woman and artist that I am today. I love sharing every moment of this journey with you. I love you more each day!

My personal editor, but more importantly, my dear friend, Nancy Wilkinson: Thank you for pre-editing and the fine critique of dashes, indents, and asterisks!

Debbie Byrne, staff, and students at Byrne Sewing Connection: You have listened and guided me through all my ups and downs; I would not want to share this sewing journey with anyone else.

The "Longstreth Moms": Who would have thought a T-shirt quilt would have led to this…

Many store owners, staff, and students: I love how our relationship has grown into a wonderful friendship.

The generosity and support from Brother USA, Mettler Threads, Northcott Fabrics, and Timeless Treasures Fabrics: Your products make my quilts shine!

My family and friends: Thank you for your love and support.

Introduction

As a child, I always loved to color. The greatest gifts I would receive were a new coloring book and a big box of crayons. But sewing is a different story. I never enjoyed sewing when I was younger. I always had trouble with the machine, bird's nests in my bobbins, and broken needles. So when I started sewing many decades later, my mother was shocked and puzzled as to why I would I want to start sewing.

Soon after I started to sew, I discovered many different colors and types of threads. I was so excited to just play! I could see the changes on the fabric when I layered the threads, added metallic threads, did bobbin work, and added embellishments. My head spun with ideas, and soon I was hooked. Now I can truly say that I love playing with threads and I love sewing, especially creating quilts with thread painting and embellishments.

Shortly after I started sewing, I was asked to teach my techniques. When I first started teaching, I would design a pattern for the class. The students would trace the design, then thread paint the project. I quickly found out that people work at different speeds and that my students were at many different stages during the class. To keep everyone together during class and save time with designing, I started to work with panels. I began to look at panels with a different eye. What can I do with them? What can I change or add? Can I teach different techniques on a specific panel? Many of the answers were yes and produced amazing results. I love how a panel no longer looks like a panel but rather a true piece of art!

My hope and purpose with this book is that you, the reader, will have the same excitement and wonderful results as I do. Try the techniques covered in this book and add your own ideas to a panel. New panels are designed every year, so try these ideas and techniques on ones that are similar to those featured in this book or, even better, mix it up and create something new and different. Create your own piece of art!

CHAPTER 1

PANELS

Why Use Panels?

When I first started to teach art quilt classes, I would design a pattern and students would trace, cut, and copy my designs. Students would then learn the numerous techniques that were used on the project. This turned out to be very time-consuming. Many of my students were at different steps during the class, causing delays, pressure to catch up with others, and sometimes frustration with the creative process itself. I would hear many students saying things like, "I am not creative," "I do not know how to design," "I am not sure what colors to use," and "Am I using the correct proportion and size of items?"

I needed a way to keep everyone in sync and allow my students to enjoy the whole learning and creating process. I wanted them to not be intimidated by the process and to be less critical of themselves as artists. So I started to look at premade panels for teaching. Panels soon became a great tool for me to teach many of my ideas and techniques while minimizing frustration for my students.

The main advantage of using a panel is that the designing process is done for you. There are many wonderful panels on the market today, and the designer's talent and knowledge of size, shape, proportion, and color are already incorporated into each panel, allowing you to save time and skip the sometimes frustrating designing steps. This will allow you to jump right into the fun part: choosing the techniques you will use to create your own unique piece of art.

You will find that many of the ideas and techniques shared in this book can be carried from one panel to another. This allows for each project to be individually created and altered as desired. When you have finished your panel, it will no longer look like a panel, but rather a unique work of art, and you will have learned and enjoyed the creative process along the way.

What Makes a Good Panel?

Now that you understand why using panels is a great idea, you are sure to go shopping for them and find many beautiful options to choose from. You may see a lovey panel and think, "This will look gorgeous when I thread paint it and add some embellishments!" Now, this might be true, but there are several considerations to think about when choosing a panel. The five considerations are:

- What is the size and detail level of the print?
- Are there any lines on the panel, vertical or horizontal?
- Is the panel an entire scenic design?
- Will the panel need a new background fabric? Why?
- Can the panel be redesigned?
  Let's look at each consideration in more detail.

What is the size and detail level of the print?

Look for designs and patterns on panels that are large and open. This allows for many techniques to be used on the panel, such as thread painting, trapunto, and three-dimensional effects. You need space and large areas on a panel for these kinds of techniques to be effective. If the design is too small, you can lose the detail of the design. This can have a negative effect on the overall panel and limit the ways in which you can incorporate additional design elements.

Are there any lines on the panel, vertical or horizontal?

Are there lines or designs on the print that create a visual line, such as inner borders, words, buildings, trees, or water? Many of

Left: The large flower petals and leaves will make this panel relatively easy to work with. Center: The dense, fine detail in this panel's main design may be hard to maintain. Right: Large, simple shapes will make this panel easy to customize.

Welcome Friends

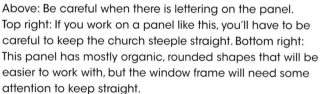

Above: Be careful when there is lettering on the panel.
Top right: If you work on a panel like this, you'll have to be careful to keep the church steeple straight. Bottom right: This panel has mostly organic, rounded shapes that will be easier to work with, but the window frame will need some attention to keep straight.

the techniques you may use will distort the panel somewhat, making continuous lines sometimes difficult to keep straight. Consider how you are going to maintain and keep these lines straight with the techniques that will be used on the panel. Will you have to quilt the lines first to stabilize the panel? Also take note of whether the panel is printed straight and if the lines can be straightened out.

Is the panel an entire scenic design?

Scenic panels make wonderful projects. Scenic panels have the correct coloring, size, and detail already done for you. If you choose to work with a scenic panel, it is best kept as a whole panel to maintain the integrity of the design. Look for large elements in the print. Remember, smaller elements can get lost when adding certain techniques.

Above: This panel, which is a featured project on page 88, has large swaths of sky, rock, water, and tree to work with.

Above: This lovely composition, featured on page 104, should be used in full to include all the elements of sky, water, grass, heron, and lilies.

Left: Be careful not to lose the details of the geese, children, and background house in this piece.

Will the panel need a new background fabric? Why?

There are a few things to consider when deciding if a project will need a new background.

Are there lines on the background print? If so, how are they going to be kept straight? If there are too many lines on the background, it might be best

Above: This tree is perfect for doing trapunto, which is best done with a new background. It is a featured project on page 76. Top right: The rigid, crisscrossing lines in the background of this panel will be a pain to deal with. Bottom right: These poppies go right up to the edge of the panel, so they are a good candidate for placing on a new background.

Left: Imagine some possibilities for this design. Perhaps you could fussy cut the individual snowflakes along the top and bottom and scatter them across a wider background. Center: This lively winter scene was redesigned using a duplicate panel to add more width and birds; it's a featured project on page 96. Right: The individual elements on this panel are ripe to be fussy cut.

to remove the main design and apply it to a new background.

Is the design very close to the edge of the panel? You can apply the main design to a new, larger background and have more room to work different techniques.

What techniques are you going to use on the panel? Techniques that may distort the panel, such as trapunto, work best when the main design is applied to a new background.

Do you want to change the overall size of the panel, whether to make it larger or smaller? Using a new background might be the easiest way to do that.

Can the panel be redesigned?

Generally, panels are meant to be one cohesive design, but can the panel be fussy cut and redesigned? Using a panel in this fashion can produce some amazing results! Can two different panels be combined together? Can a duplicate of a single panel be mined for additional pieces to add to the original panel? Don't be afraid to think outside the box.

CHAPTER 2

GETTING STARTED

Supplies

Once you have selected your panel, it is time to get your supplies ready. Listed in this section are the supplies that will be needed to complete the various projects throughout this book. Many are used on all the projects, and some supplies are only used for specific techniques.

Sewing Machine

All of the projects seen throughout this book were completed on a domestic sewing machine. The machine does not need to be the newest, biggest, and best to complete the projects in this book, but some features are necessary and very helpful. Here are the features I look for:

- The machine needs to be able to do free-motion quilting with a straight and zigzag stitch. When doing free-motion quilting and thread painting, the feed dogs need to be dropped to allow the fabric to move freely under the foot.
- Look for a large throat space between the needle and the machine housing on the right. A larger space gives you extra room to maneuver the fabric. When there is less bulk, drag, and pull on the fabric, a smoother stitch is created.
- You will want the ability to use different feet, such as open-toe, free-motion, couching, and fringe feet.
- You will want the ability to do bobbin work and work with thicker threads. I encourage a spare bobbin case to allow for the adjustment of bobbin tension.

Dropped feed dogs

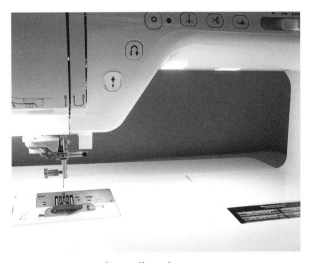

Large throat space

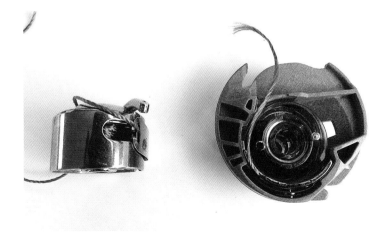

A spare bobbin case

Machine Feet

Several different feet are used throughout this book. Each has its own purpose for effect and technique. A free-motion foot allows for your fabric to move freely while quilting. An open-toe foot has a wide opening, and is often used for decorative stitching and adding embellishments. A fringe foot works with a zigzag stitch to create stiches that are dimensional. A couching foot allows you to sew with thick yarns and threads.

Threads

There are so many threads in the quilting market that you can easily get confused, wondering what they all are and when to use them. Threads differ by weight, type, ply, color, and purpose. I will focus here on the threads that I use for my quilting, thread painting, and different techniques.

The most important concern to me is the thread weight and type. Thread weights are measured by the thickness of the thread. Ranging from 12 weight to 100 weight, the

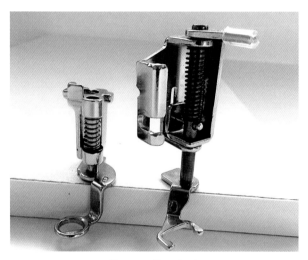

Free-motion foot

Fringe foot

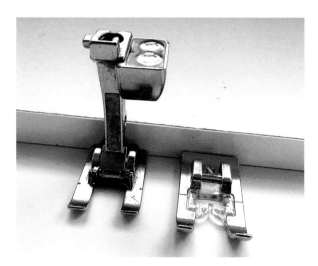

Open-toe foot

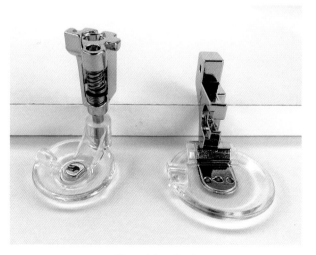

Couching foot

Use thinner threads for free-motion quilting.

I like to free-motion quilt with thin threads in large, open areas like skies.

lower the number, the thicker the thread. So, 40 weight threads are thicker than 50 weight threads, and 50 weight threads are thicker than 60 weight threads. I also go by the appearance and feel of the thread. Given two threads of the same listed weight, one may look or feel thicker than the other.

I also consider the type of thread. I prefer cottons or cotton blends for the top threads and polyester for the bobbin threads, but this is not a hard and fast rule.

Here are some specific threads I use over and over:

For free-motion quilting: I use Mettler® Metrosene® or Mettler Poly Sheen®, which are thin-weight polyester threads. I will use a thinner thread when I want the stitching to be less visible and not the main focus on the project. Areas I free-motion quilt are usually backgrounds, skies, and/or open areas.

For thread painting: For top threads, I use Mettler Silk-Finish Cotton 50 weight thread, both in solids and variegated colors. This cotton medium-weight thread has a nice feel and a slightly thicker appearance. The stitching shows up very well and allows for nice shading and

Use slightly thicker threads for thread painting.

Thread painting has added a lot of color and texture to this pumpkin and flower.

blending of thread colors. For bobbin thread, I use a thinner weight polyester thread, such as Mettler Poly Sheen. I try to balance the weights so the project will not get too stiff or distorted. Also, metallic threads are wonderful for added effects such as a shine on leaves or sparkle on water. Adding metallic threads creates many interesting results.

For bobbin work: Bobbin work is done when the threads are too thick to fit through the eye of the needle. The thick threads are placed in the bobbin and the project is sewn on the backside so that the heavier threads are seen on the top of the project. I tend to use very thick threads such as YLI Jeans Stitch, pearl/perle cotton, and braided metal threads, as well as yarn and ribbons.

Bobbin work is made for thick, chunky threads.

The berries here were enhanced with standout bobbin work.

Metal Thread Stand

I find stands to be very helpful when using many different threads and spools. If you can't remember if the thread should be placed on the vertical or horizontal spindle, just use a thread stand! The stand is placed behind the machine, helping the thread to relax and come off the spool evenly, preventing thread breakage.

Thread stand

Needles

Using the correct thread is very important, but equally important is using the correct needle. Nothing is more frustrating than your thread fraying or breaking, skipping stiches, or needles breaking. You need to match the correct size and type of needle for the different threads that

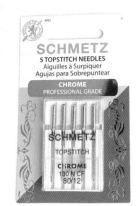

Use the right needle for the right job.

are being used. When the correct combination of thread and needle is used, you will have a better stitch and more success with sewing.

I highly recommend having several packs of needles on hand when starting a new project. When you are thread painting, you will go through many layers of fabric and threads. The needle is penetrating through all these layers, causing the point to dull over time. A dull point means the sewing machine has to work harder to create the stitches. Often, a dull point will cause skipped stitches and broken threads. I recommend changing the needle when thread problems arise and after four to five hours of high-density stitching.

Free-motion quilting: I use a Schmetz Topstitch 80/12 needle. A topstitch 80/12 needle has a deeper groove, which provides more protection for the thread; it also has a large eye, which is good for free-motion quilting. An 80/12 needle works well for light to medium stitch density, such as background quilting, skies, and the like. This size needle creates smaller holes in the fabric and is less visible. An 80/12 needle matched with Mettler Poly Sheen or Mettler Metrosene thread (or any thinner polyester thread) creates a beautiful stitch.

Thread painting: I use a Schmetz Topstitch 90/14 needle. A topstitch 90/14 needle has a slightly thicker blade than an 80/12 needle, making it stronger. I will increase the needle size to accommodate thicker threads and the dense stitching of thread painting. The thicker threads and the motion of thread painting while blending and shading can cause extra pull on the needle. A 90/14 needle matched with Mettler Silk-Finish Cotton 50 (or any cotton medium-weight thread) works wonderfully for thread painting. If your threads continue to break or fray, increase the needle size to 100/16.

Batting and Muslin

I use cotton batting (Warm and Natural® brand is my favorite) layered with a light-colored cotton muslin on all my projects. I layer the muslin, batting, and fabric panel in that order. The batting and muslin act as a stabilizer and solid foundation for quilting, thread painting, and the numerous techniques covered in this book. This stabilization is needed to help reduce or eliminate puckering, stitch distortion, and shrinkage.

I always use both batting and muslin in my quilting projects to stabilize and prevent distortion.

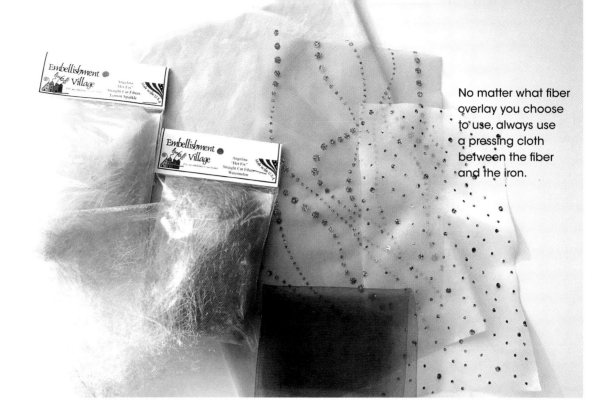

No matter what fiber overlay you choose to use, always use a pressing cloth between the fiber and the iron.

Adhesives

You will use different products for different reasons, but they all have the same purpose: adhering two fabrics or fibers together. Here are three key products.

Fusible web: This is used when panels have been fussy cut and need to be adhered to a new background. It is thin-weight sheet, which is best for a sewable bond and allowing fabrics to keep their soft feel. It is a permanent bond. I often use HeatnBond Lite®.

Basting adhesive: This spray adhesive is used to adhere layers of fabric together. It eliminates pinning and creates a temporary bond. I often use SpraynBond®.

Liquid craft/fabric adhesive: This is a permanent liquid adhesive that is used for a quick bond to adhere fabrics and embellishments together. I often use Fabric Fuse™.

Overlays and Pressing Cloths

There are many fiber overlays you can incorporate into your projects, such as tulle, organza, and hot fix fibers (sold as Angelina fibers and sometimes as "fantasy fibers"). Most overlays are sheer fabrics layered over portions of your project to add depth, texture, and dimension. When an overlay is added to a project, a pressing cloth is needed to prevent burning and/or melting of the fibers.

Depending on your exact need, you will choose one of a variety of different adhesive products.

Rulers

When marking and squaring a quilt, I use the largest ruler possible. I love my 20½" x 20½" (52 x 52cm) ruler. It allows you to check several lines (vertical and horizontal) on the panel at one time. More reference lines allow you to square a project perfectly.

Marking Tools

There are plenty of marking tools on the market. The marking tools I use are pencils and chalk. For all marking tools, test on scrap fabric prior to marking your projects. Some colors are harder to remove and can leave a residue. Pencils and chalk can be used to square a quilt and mark free-motion quilting designs.

Embellishments

You can never have too many embellishments! Embellishments can include beads, buttons, ribbons, trims, crystals, and more. These are the finishing touches added to any project. Sometimes an embellishment can pull the whole project together, truly completing the look.

Above: Visit your local fabric store to explore the variety of embellishments they have on the shelves.

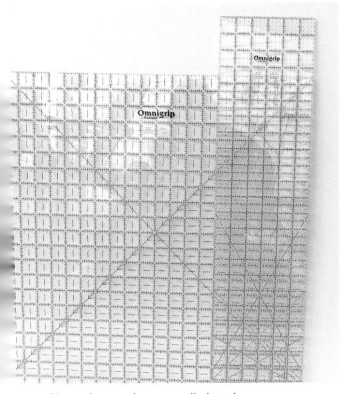

Above: Large rulers are quite handy.

Right: Test out different marking tools to find what works for you and the particular fabric you are using.

Prepping for a Panel Project

Selecting and Preparing a New Background

As discussed in Chapter 1, a new background may be needed for your art quilt. There may be too many lines in the background, the design may be printed crookedly on the fabric, the design may be too close to the edge of the panel, or the design might simply be too large or too small for your taste. The easiest way to handle these problems is to place the main design onto a new background.

When using a new background, **cut the new background a few inches (several centimeters) larger** than the desired finished size. This will allow for distortion and shrinkage.

When the design is quite detailed and the original panel background can be seen throughout the design, try to **match the new background** to the original panel background as much as possible. If they are matched well enough, the two will blend together. Then fussy cut the outer edge of the design off of the panel. This will save time and you will not lose any detail of the design.

This new background is very similar to the existing background, which means it will blend easily against this detailed design.

Some panels just have **too many lines**, but the main design is beautiful. It is easier to use a new background and not deal with the lines and frustration that comes with trying to quilt while keeping lines straight. If the original panel background is not mixed within the design, you can use any color for the new background.

If a design is **very close to the edge of the panel**, a new background is probably needed. Thread painting and many techniques will distort the shape of the panel. A new and

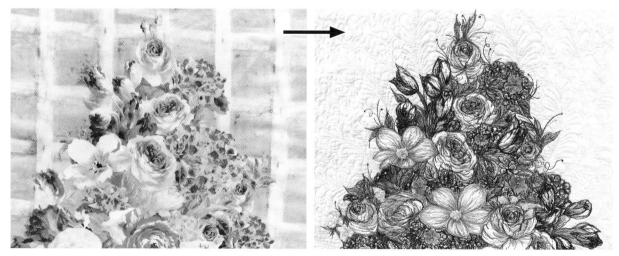

These background lines are sure to become a source of frustration if kept. Avoid the problem by using a new, solid color background.

This is a beautiful design, but it's very close to the edge of the panel. A new background adds plenty of breathing room.

This delightful bird scene is full of interesting detail, but is very vertical and a bit stiff with its structured left column. Look at the result when a duplicate of the panel is mined for additional birds and the design is widened out on a new, organic background.

larger background allows for this distortion and has plenty of fabric to square up the quilt without cutting into your work.

Don't be afraid to **totally redesign a panel**, either. Some panels were designed with the intent to make something specific, such as an apron; others are extremely busy or extremely large. Don't overlook these panels as options for your art. Look at the main design on the panel and see if it can possibly be rearranged into a unique piece with a more pleasing design. You can customize the size and design to fit your personal tastes. Be creative and think past the original design.

Adding Adhesive to a Panel

Once you have decided that a panel needs a new background, the next step is to adhere the main design to the new background. You will find it easier to apply fusible web before you fussy cut your design. That way, you can extend the adhesive onto the old background and not have to worry about precise placement of the adhesive along a detailed edge.

1. If a design is small, it is easier to apply the fusible web to cover the whole piece. Place the adhesive on the entire back side of the panel and iron to adhere, following the manufacturer's instructions (do not remove the paper backing on the exposed side). If a design is larger, cut the adhesive into 1½" (3.8cm) strips and only apply them to the outside edges of the design. Since the design is being kept whole and in one piece, the center does not need the adhesive, and you will save on fusible web.

2. Cut around the outside of the design.

3. Remove the backing paper from the adhesive.

4. Place the design on the new background, making sure you have enough space on all four sides. Iron the design in place.

Layering the Project

To prepare a project, you need to make a **quilt sandwich**. A quilt sandwich consists of three layers: muslin, batting, and a top fabric (the original panel or new assembled background). Always cut the muslin and batting 3" (7.6cm) larger than the top fabric on all four sides. For example, if your panel is 20" x 24" (50.8 x 61cm), cut the muslin and batting to 26" x 30" (66 x 76.2cm). The extra muslin and batting acts as a stabilizer and helps prevent some distortion and shrinkage. It also allows greater flexibility for finishing the project—you can add borders, a binding, or additional batting later.

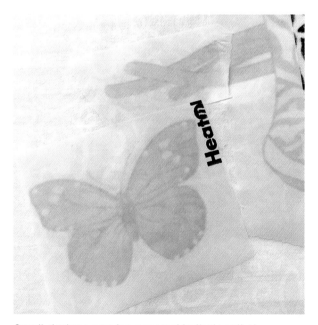

Use strips of adhesive to cover only the edges of large designs to avoid waste and stiffness on the quilt.

Small designs can be covered in their entirety with adhesive.

A quilt sandwich consists of two larger layers of muslin and batting under the top fabric.

For small projects and wall hangings, which includes all the projects and panels in this book, **spray baste** the quilt sandwich. The purpose of basting is to keep all three layers flat together without shifting or pleating. Basting adhesive temporarily holds the layers together. If needed, this allows for repositioning while working on the project. Work in a well-ventilated or outside area while spraying, and follow the manufacturer's instructions.

1. Prior to basting, iron all three layers to remove all wrinkles.

2. Spray baste the muslin and batting together.

3. Place the panel or assembled background fabric in the center of the basted muslin and batting. Pull the top half of the panel down and spray the panel. Then press the panel flat onto the batting with your hands. Repeat with the bottom half of the panel. If the panel or project is larger, it is best to work in thirds.

First spray and press down the top half.

Then spray and press down the bottom half.

CHAPTER 3

TECHNIQUES

The techniques in this chapter are generally presented in the order in which you would want to implement them while working on a project. Occasionally, some techniques are partially finished and then completed after other steps are completed. For example, you might do some thread painting, followed by a tulle overlay, and then finish with more thread painting. Review all the instructions for all the techniques you want to use before proceeding with a project, to make sure you can plan ahead as necessary.

Free-Motion Quilting

There are many wonderful books on the market written about how to free-motion quilt. I will cover the basics on how but will primarily focus on the why, when, and where to free-motion quilt when working with a panel and completing a project.

How to Free-Motion Quilt

First, get everything set up. Clear the sewing area of items such as scissors, threads, and fabrics. You want the quilt to be as weightless as possible, with no pull or drag on the fabric. Drop the sewing machine feed dogs to allow the fabric to move freely under the foot (check your machine manual). You will need a free-motion foot (see page 14). I like to use a closed-toe foot; this prevents the threads from getting caught on the foot opening (especially when thread painting). Plastic or metal feet both work well, but the visibility of the needle is important. Have the machine set in the needle down position. When you need to stop and/ or reposition the fabric, a straighter stitch is formed when restarting with the needle down.

When starting to free-motion quilt, take one stitch in place and stop to pull up the bobbin thread. Now take two to three small stitches backward and sew over the first stitch to secure the threads. Stop and clip the threads.

While free-motion quilting, you need to coordinate the speed of the machine, the pressure on the foot pedal, and the movement of the fabric. If your machine can be operated without the foot pedal, try it! That is one less thing to worry about while perfecting your stitching. Don't be afraid to free-motion quilt a little faster than your normal speed. Play around with the motor speed and moving the fabric to find the perfect combination for you.

When everything is working together, you can hear your machine hum!

Typically, if the fabric is moved too quickly, big, open stitches are formed, and if the fabric is moved too slowly, tiny, small stitches are formed. The goal is to create nice, evenly spaced stitches. Remember to take breaks to rest and relax your brain and muscles. When stopping to rest or reposition, stop at a point at which you can restart easily and not notice possible stop/ restarts. For less visibility of stitches and fewer tension issues, use a thin-weight thread on the top and in the bobbin that match the color of the fabric.

When free-motion quilting, you will usually want the thread to closely match the fabric.

Why, When, and Where to Free-Motion Quilt

The final look of a project is very important. The finished project should be flat, there should be no puckers or tucks, all lines should be straight, and the project should be square. How you achieve that final appearance is often determined by the decisions you make at the very beginning of your project. Look at the panel and ask yourself the following questions: How am I going to keep this flat? How am I going to keep lines (such as a horizon line) straight? What will happen to the fabric when I add additional threads and techniques later? How will I prevent distortion?

Many of these issues can be dealt with by first free-motion quilting certain areas on the project—usually the background. Free-motion quilting (in addition to the batting and muslin) will act as a stabilizer and allow for other thread work to be added later with less concern.

When the background is quilted first, there is less distortion and puckering along the edges of the design. Backgrounds should be quilted with an open and flowing pattern. It is best to blend the free-motion quilting about two or three stitches into the edge of the main motif itself. Don't worry about a little bit of thread on the design; it will get covered with other threads and embellishments.

If you add heavy and thicker threads to a panel first, you will have puckering on the outer edge of the design, which is then harder to flatten out. If you only free-motion quilt around the very outer edges of the design, a bubble will form between the design and the background. Do not quilt too close and tight, as that will make the quilt shrink and become distorted and stiff.

Top left: correct amount of quilting. Top right: no quilting prior to thread painting; notice the puckering. Bottom right: not quilted to the edge of the design, creating a bubble along the edge of the design. Bottom left: quilting is sloppy and too tight, creating stiffness and shrinkage of the background.

Quilt outward from the design.

On large, open areas, such as a new or open background, start free-motion quilting along the edges of the design nearest the center of the design and quilt from the center out.

Skies with a horizontal line or panels with images such as buildings should be free-motion quilted from the inner edge of the sky/design and pushed up and out to the sides. This will help to keep the lines straight. If you start from the top and quilt down toward the design, the lines can be pushed unevenly.

One of the hardest parts of free-motion quilting is deciding what pattern to quilt. Use the print on the panel to your advantage. For

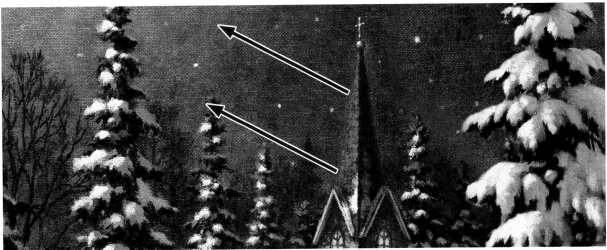

Quilt outward from straight lines like horizons and buildings.

Imitate the swirls of the clouds in this background.

Follow the subtle lines of the background flowers and leaves here.

example, skies may have clouds, and grassy fields may have flowers—follow these. If there is not a pattern to copy, consider doing an open and airy pattern. Try not to choose a pattern with a set repeat; when the pattern is off, the mistake is obvious. It will also be harder to blend in additional quilting later if needed when completing the project.

Thread Painting

One of the best ways to make an art quilt pop is to add some thread painting. Thread painting is just like it sounds: painting with thread! The needle is your brush and the threads are your paint. The threads are used to add color, highlights, and detail, while the quilting on the batting and muslin and the additional layers of fibers and threads create texture, depth, and dimension. Thread painting is done using free-motion stitching, using several different stitches and layering multiple threads and fibers. It may look and sound complicated, but it is easier than you think, and when you honor

the process, you will be rewarded with an amazingly beautiful and detailed work of art.

Thread Selection

Thread selection is very important. When picking **top threads**, use the colors on the panel as a guide. This helps you to choose the correct color tone and value. With thread painting, you will want the colors to blend into the work instead of contrasting it. I usually work with Mettler Silk-Finish Cotton 50 in variegated and solid colors.

I use **variegated threads** as my base in blending thread painting. When choosing a variegated thread, notice if there are different shades of one color or if there are multiple colors. I tend to choose variegated threads with several shades of one single color. When working on nature and landscape projects, the blending of shades from one color looks more natural. When there are several colors in the variegation, chances are the colors will stitch out in the wrong places. When choosing variegated threads, place the threads over the area to be stitched. Be cautious of threads being too extreme in color value. You do not want very light-colored threads stitched onto dark fabric or vice versa. Look for a mixed blend between the fabric and variegated threads, blending the lights and darks together. For added depth in an area, choose two different variegated threads. For example, in an area with several evergreen trees, stitch some trees with one variegated green thread and the remaining trees with a different variegated green thread. If the whole area is stitched with all the same threads, the project will often look a bit flat.

Once the variegated threads are chosen and stitched on the panel, I select the **solid threads**, in both normal cotton and metallic tones. Solid colors shade, highlight, and define a design. Working with two to four colors in a color family helps to achieve the proper effects of thread painting. The additional threads create a smooth and gradual blend of colors.

To select solid colors, place the solid threads on the sewn area. Pick the lightest solid color represented in the medium variegated color. The next solid color should be a shade or two darker, and so on, until all the solid colors are picked. If the solid colors blend too much into the variegated threads and fabric, choose one shade darker and go from there. You will almost always want to go darker rather than lighter.

Lastly, choose a **metallic thread** color to blend in with the solid colors but still create a fun and subtle sparkly highlight. Using a metallic thread is one of the best ways to really make your thread painting stand out.

For the **bobbin threads**, I often use Mettler Poly Sheen. It is a polyester thread that is stronger and thinner than the cotton threads used on the top. It is best to use a thinner weight on the bottom to balance out the thread thickness. If both top and bottom threads are thick, this will create stiffness and distortion in the project. Match the bottom thread with the color family of the top threads.

These two different variegated green threads add blended dimension to a set of otherwise identical evergreen trees.

After painting with variegated thread, move on to solid colors.

The dark green bobbin thread at left matches the color family of all the top threads.

This prevents having to adjust the machine tension. If the bottom thread does peek through on top, it will eventually be covered with additional threads and blended together.

Stitching Basics

Once you have picked out your threads, it's time to paint. This is the exciting part, the part where you start to bring your panel to life. You will use a variety of stitches and threads, layered one after the other, and each will bring more definition and dimension to your panel. Much like the layers of paint used to create a work of art, you will be amazed at how these layers will transform your panel into something beautiful and uniquely yours.

Remember these basic tips when thread painting:

- Thread painting is done in free motion; the free-motion foot is on and the feed dogs are dropped.
- Match the bobbin thread (in a thinner weight) with the color family of the top threads.

- I recommend using a Schmetz Topstitch 90/14 needle or similar.

A big concern of adding thread painting to a panel or project is the density of your stitching. The thread work and layering of multiple threads can cause distortion and puckering. A good way to get control of the puckering is to sew only in small sections and complete the stitching in each area before moving to another area. It is best not to bounce around the quilt.

You also do not want to go heavy with your first layer of threads. The first layer, zigzag stitching, is a stabilizing and blending base that will allow additional layers of thread to be added. After all the base variegated threads have been sewn, additional layers of solid threads are added for shading and definition.

During the steps of thread painting, the quilt may get wrinkled, bumpy, and distorted. If this happens, try to iron the quilt as flat as possible. I would rather iron the quilt between each step than try to sew through bumps and wrinkles. Occasional ironing will also help keep the quilt straight and flat, making it easier to square the quilt at the end.

Step 1: Zigzag Stitch with Variegated Threads

- Suggested thread: Mettler Silk-Finish Cotton 50
- Change the machine settings to a width of 2.0 and a length of 0.0 (or the lowest length the machine will go). If the design is small, decrease the width to 1.5.
- Complete all zigzag sewing with variegated threads on the entire panel before adding solid threads with straight stitching.
- The stitching in this first step is used to stabilize the quilt for additional stitching.
- Pick thread colors from the colors on the panel.

Step 2: Straight Stitch with Solid Threads

- Suggested thread: Mettler Silk-Finish Cotton 50 and/or metallic threads
- Do not change the stitch width or length.
- Pick solid colors from the colors in the variegated threads.

- For shading and detail stitching, work from the lightest-color threads to the darkest. The only exception is for metallic threads—these should be used prior to the darkest color.

Zigzag Stitching

Zigzag stitching is the first step of the thread painting process. The stitching should be sewn on all the edges of the design and also inside it to blend and add shading.

Place the area to be sewn on a horizontal axis and sew side to side, left to right. Move

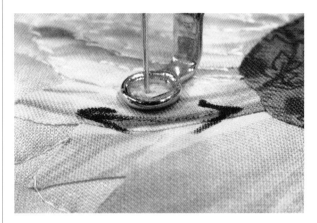

The drawn arrow in this photo shows the sewing direction.

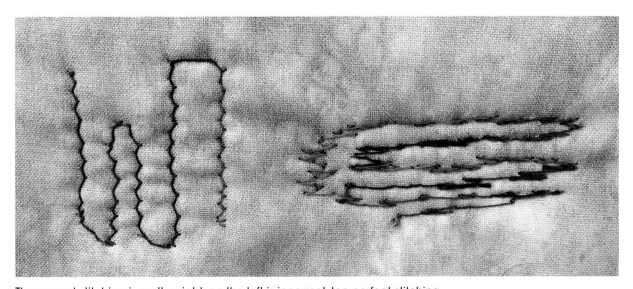

The correct stitching is on the right; on the left is incorrect, too-perfect stitching.

the fabric in a rocking back-and-forth motion, creating a serrated line that almost looks like a straight stitch. The stitching should not actually look like a true zigzag; you do not want the stitch to be uniform in length. The serration of the stitch creates a nice blending of the variegated threads—you cannot see the continuous repeat of color changes in the thread.

Have the machine set in the needle-down position, allowing you to easily pivot and realign the fabric in the correct direction when needed. Don't forget to pivot the fabric if/when the design changes direction.

Zigzag stitching at this stage is a great way to handle raw edge appliqué. The serrated stitching will catch the edges and helps prevent fraying of the fabric.

Zigzag stitching catches all the edges of any raw edge appliqué.

Straight Stitching

Straight stitching is done after the base variegated zigzag stitching is completed. The straight stitching is sewn in multiple layers of threads. Sew from lightest to darkest in color, working with two to four thread colors per motif (leaf, flower, etc.). When working on a panel that has many of the same motif, try to mix up the thread layering. This will create depth in the quilt and prevent a flat look where everything has identical threads. For example, if you have

Light thread adds highlights.

Metallic thread adds a bit of sparkle.

The darkest thread adds shading.

Here is the entire collection of threads used on these leaves, in order from left to right.

Here are some other examples of stitched leaves. Note the color choices.

three leaves, choose four threads to use, and work one leaf with all four, one leaf with three, and the last leaf with a different three.

The **lighter-colored threads** are used first, and serve to accent and highlight an area, adding details like veins on the leaves.

If you are using **metallic threads**, sew with them next, before the darkest color. Add them where an extra sparkle or highlight may be needed. To sew successfully with metallic threads, sew at half speed and use a thread stand. The stand allows the thread to relax and unwind prior to going through the tension disc.

Use the **darkest thread** to shade and define the design. Incorporate it in every motif.

Samples

Below are a few samples of items where I either fussy cut or used solid fabric to show the direction and detail of the stitching. Described here are the steps of layering the threads to get the desired effects, and where and when other possible techniques may be added.

Both of these flowers were made with identical yellow and brown fabric bases. The difference is the color of threads used. The thread choice dramatically affects the final result.

The numbers indicate the number of solid color threads used in that area—two, three, or four colors.

The numbers indicate the number of solid color threads used in that area—two, three, or four colors.

Flowers

Flowers are a common motif that are good for practice.

1. Zigzag stitch (width 2.0, length 0.0) with variegated yellow thread on the petals. Cover the outer edges of the petals and some stitching inside near the center of the flower.

2. Zigzag stitch (width 2.0, length 0.0) with variegated brown thread in small circles to fill the center.

3. Straight stitch along the petals and add some stitching inside for additional detail and shading. Layer from lightest to darkest threads. If using metallic thread, add before the darkest thread.

Step 2

4. Complete the center as desired. In the sample, the left flower was completed with straight stitch dark brown circles; the right flower was completed with bobbin work (see page 48).

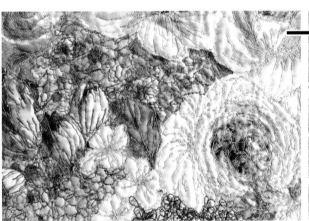

Zigzag stitch applied

Straight stitch applied

Zigzag stitch applied

Straight stitch applied

Evergreens

This sample is sewn straight onto blue fabric. These steps would be followed on a panel with evergreen trees.

1. Zigzag stitch (width 2.0, length 0.0) in variegated green. (When actually working on a panel, use the shape and branches as a guide.) Sew from the top, dropping down in layers to create the branching on the tree. It is fine to overlap the branches; this actually looks more natural. Remember to hold the fabric on a horizontal angle to get a serrated line.

2. If there are multiple trees on the panel, use two different variegated threads, one per tree, to create depth.

3. If you want to add overlay (see page 42) for snow, add it before proceeding to the solid threads.

4. Straight stitch with a medium green. Sew on the branches and make needles over the prior zigzag stitching. Mix up the colors for added depth.

5. Straight stitch with dark green on all the branches. Sew up the branches to make the stem, and then go down the sides to add more needles.

6. If you added an overlay, stitch over the overlay with the two greens. This will create a natural layering.

This evergreen has had jewel embellishments added for extra glimmer (see page 55).

A glittery overlay of snow has been incorporated among these evergreen boughs.

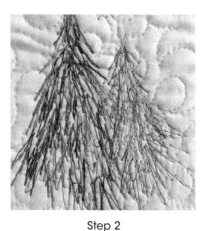

Step 2

Step 4

Step 5

Here are some gorgeous examples of stone and wood textures within scenes. Note how the stitch lines reflect the natural personality of the material, with rounder lines for the stones and sharper lines for the wood fence.

Wood and Stone

Wood and stone often appear in the form of tree trunks, fences, and buildings.

1. Zigzag stitch (width 2.0, length 0.0) with a variegated brown in the direction of the grain.

2. Straight stitch with a solid medium brown; add some shading, but not all over the design.

3. Straight stitch with a solid dark brown; use it to shade and add additional detail and definition to the area.

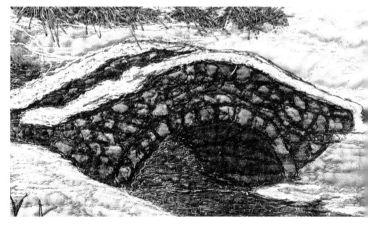

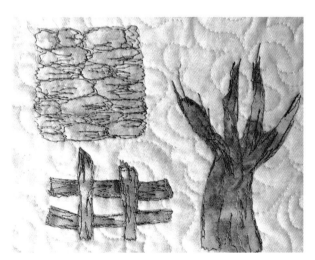

Step 1

Step 3

Notice how the simple stitching of branches or curlicues flattens the open background areas.

Finishing

When all the quilting, thread painting, and other techniques are finished, the quilt will need to be ironed flat. Occasionally there are some areas, such as the sky, background, or areas not evenly thread painted, that will have a bump or bubble. What do you do? All you need to do is add some stitching over the bubble. Add a whimsical curlicue, branches, grasses, or free-motion quilt over it. But if you add a curlicue in one place, add some more elsewhere in the quilt so it looks balanced.

Trapunto

Trapunto is a quilting technique that creates a raised and puffy surface. This is achieved when an open area is surrounded by outline stitching/quilting, and the open area is slit on the back and stuffed.

Trapunto can be used on any quilt, but should it? When working with panels, you will want to consider the effect it will have on your project. How will it blend in? What will trapunto add to the quilt? Can the quilt benefit from the added dimension? Some panels need items to pop or appear more in the foreground, and trapunto can help achieve this. On other panels, it may be overkill. Remember, sometimes less is more; you do not need to use every technique on every quilt.

This dinosaur looms out at you.

The puffy Christmas ornaments make you want to touch this tree design.

This entire tree has been lightly stuffed.

A soft trapunto bird is an interesting contrast to the stitched surroundings.

Supplies

- Lightweight fusible stabilizer
- Polyfill stuffing or batting
- Free-motion foot

1. Layer the quilt: muslin, batting, and panel/background.

2. Mark the area for trapunto. Since most areas of the quilt have already been free-motion quilted or thread painted, the general marking of an area has likely been done already. But the exact shape and space needs to be marked for stuffing, and that is done with stitching. On the top of the quilt, free-motion stitch a line around the area where trapunto will be used.

3. Make a small slit on the muslin within the marked area.

4. Fill the area with polyfill or batting until it is nice and smooth on the front. Be careful not to overstuff.

Step 3

Step 6

Back

Front

Step 7

Very dense stitching from quilting or thread painting will create more bunching and distortion on the area that is not quilted. This may be hard to fill smoothly and may require extra stuffing.

5. Cover the slit with lightweight fusible stabilizer and iron to adhere to the muslin. It is fine to have the stabilizer cover the whole area that has been filled.

6. Re-stitch around the area to secure the stabilizer.

7. Additional inside stiches may be added after stuffing and closing the slit for more added detail.

Be aware that if there is too much stuffing, you may not be able to move the foot and/or it will be hard to sew through the fabric. If this occurs, remove some stuffing. Also, too much additional sewing after stuffing will cause the area to become flat and undo the raised effect you were aiming for.

Overlay

One of my favorite techniques to create texture and dimension on a panel is to incorporate an overlay. An overlay is another fiber layered and sewn on top of the panel. It can be tulle, netting, organza, hot fix (Angelina) fibers, or something else. Overlays come in numerous colors and effects; they can be sheer or opaque, matte or shiny, and with or without sparkles. The possibilities are endless! You can always find the perfect overlay to create your desired effect.

Overlays can be made of tulle, netting, and many other fabrics and fibers.

Always use a pressing cloth when ironing quilts that have had any overlays added on them. Many popular overlays, including hot fix (Angelina) fibers, will melt and burn if heat is directly applied to them.

Supplies

- Overlay fabrics/fibers, such as organza, tulle, or hot fix (Angelina) fibers
- Threads matching the overlay colors
- Pressing cloth
- Iron
- Free-motion foot

1. Cut the overlay slightly larger than the area to be covered. Place the overlay on top of the desired area.

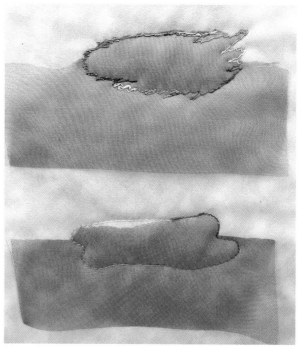

2. With a small zigzag free-motion stitch, sew along the edge of the design. Use a zigzag stitch in order to catch all the fine fibers on the edges and allow for trimming (shown top). If a straight stich is used in this step, the overlay will not be securely attached to the panel when the excess overlay is trimmed (shown bottom).

3. Carefully trim around the outside edges of the overlay. Do not cut inside the overlay or threads.

4. Add additional stitching, thread painting, and/or bobbin work along the edges to blend in the overlay. See the rest of the photos in this section for ideas.

Making a Sheet of Hot Fix (Angelina) Fibers

1. Place the hairlike hot fix fibers between two pressing cloths.

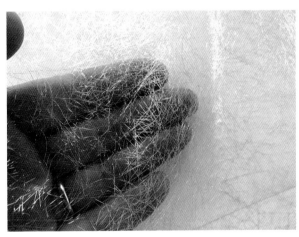

2. Iron for approximately three to five seconds until the fibers are bonded together and become a shiny sheet of "fabric."

3. Place the shiny sheet over the desired area and free-motion quilt as desired. Sew carefully, keeping the sheet flat while sewing.

4. Trim excess as needed.

Ideas for Using Organza, Tulle, and Hot Fix (Angelina) Fibers

Snow

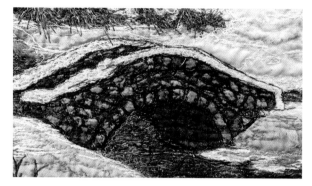

Adding a layer of organza helps to achieve a look of new-fallen snow, creating a realistic shimmer of snow on top of roofs, branches, and the like. Look for organza that has sparkles on it. The added shine looks beautiful.

Use two layers of overlay, and layer the darker piece underneath to create depth and shading.

Mix organza and tulle to create texture and depth, as done in the snow here. This is great for shading.

Use a light blue overlay with sparkles to help distinguish a specific area, such as the edge of this ice.

Sky

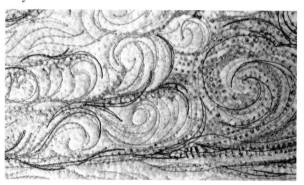

A sheet of hot fix (Angelina) fibers works beautifully to create a sparkling sky. The very sheer, iridescent, and thin layer adds the perfect effect, while still allowing the fabric design to show through.

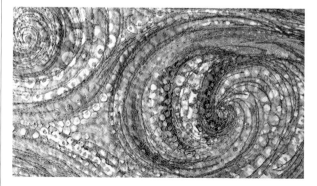

Very sparingly, use a sparkly organza to form swirls and/or clouds in the sky.

Water

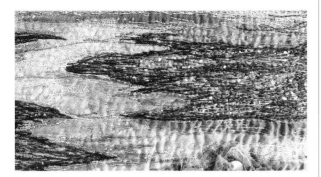

Mix organza and white tulle to create shallow water and splashes.

If the organza has sparkles or a design, place the sparkles/design in the direction of the water flow. In this piece, the top part has been completed with additional thread painting; the bottom shows the overlay with sparkles.

To create the reflection of light on the water, intermix a white or iridescent organza with several blues.

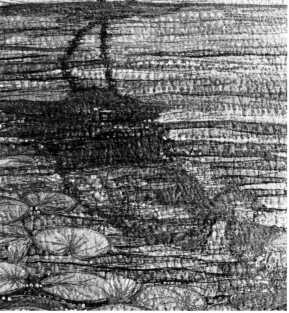

Depth and shadowing on the water is created when two overlay layers are used and overlapped.

Three-Dimensional Effects

There are times when the quilting and thread painting you have completed looks great but there is still something missing—the quilt looks flat. So you think, "If I add more threads, that will make the quilt pop!" But then you get the opposite result: The quilt looks even flatter and less interesting. This may be the time to add a three-dimensional quilted element to the quilt. Three-dimensional quilting can bring an image forward and help create depth in a quilt. To create these layers and dimension, a second panel is typically needed as a source of matching fabric.

Adding a three-dimensional element is one of the last steps to be completed during a project. Prior to adding three-dimensional pieces, all quilting, overlays, and thread painting should be finished. It is also easier to square up a quilt and get temporary measurements when the ruler is flat to the quilt—that is, before adding any three-dimensional elements.

Supplies

- Additional panel or fabric
- Lightweight fusible stabilizer
- Scrap fabrics
- Free-motion foot

1. Iron lightweight fusible stabilizer on the back side of the additional panel or fabric, overlaying the desired designs with an extra margin of ½" (1.5cm) all around. Cut each design element off the panel, maintaining the ½" (1.5cm) margin all around the design.

Though it can be hard to see in a photo, each of these three designs has a three-dimensional element that adds interesting depth to the quilt.

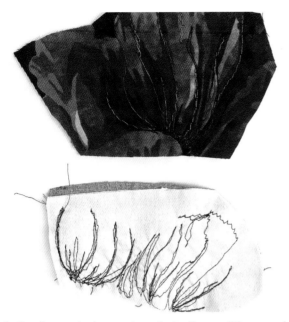

2. On the cut elements, mimic the quilting and thread painting steps that were done on the main design.

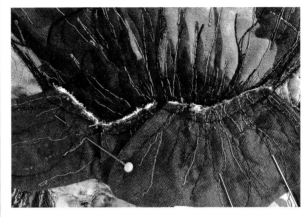

3. Using colored scrap fabric that matches the elements, place the fabrics' right sides together and sew around the edge, leaving an opening. Then turn right side out.

4. Press and close the opening.

5. Add additional quilting. This will add detail and help to mold the piece when attaching it to the quilt.

6. Place the element on top of the panel, checking for proper placement.

7. With the back side facing up, pin it where you want it to be attached. If needed, tuck and pleat the piece to fit the size and shape desired.

8. Sew very close to the edge of the element to attach it to the quilt.

9. Flip the element over to the right side. Tuck and sew where desired to secure it in its final position. Be careful not to sew the whole piece down to the quilt—leave open spaces to create layers and dimension. This allows you to hide the edges and create a nice finish.

Machine Techniques

A great way to add texture and dimension to a quilt is by playing with the bobbin and the different feet for your machine. Blend the stitching with assorted threads to create a fun and textured appearance. Here are three different machine techniques you can mix and match.

Bobbin Work

When you want to use beautiful specialty threads like jeans, pearl cottons, silk ribbons, and yarn, you will need to do bobbin work, because the threads are too thick to go through the eye of the needle. In bobbin work, the specialty thread is wound onto the bobbin and the stitching is done with the right side of the fabric facing down. You can do bobbin work in straight sewing using decorative stitches or using free-motion stitching. At first it looks and sounds complicated, but if you understand the process and follow the proper steps, it really isn't hard at all. Bobbin work gives some spectacular effects and is well worth trying!

First, let's go over some tips and things to consider.

Bobbin cases: There are two types of bobbin cases: drop-in bobbin cases, which load from the top, and removable bobbin cases, which are inserted into the machine from the front or side. Since the thicker threads need to be placed in the bobbin, the bobbin case will need to be loosened and adjusted. Once you have adjusted the tension for bobbin work, you will need to readjust the tension back for regular sewing. For this reason, I recommend having a spare bobbin case that you use exclusively for your bobbin work. I marked mine with red marker so I wouldn't forget.

Don't let yourself be limited—use bobbin work to take advantage of fun specialty threads.

I used red marker to mark a spare bobbin case for use exclusively in my bobbin work.

Adjusting tension on the bobbin case: Read your manual for making adjustments. If the threads need to be pulled and yanked out of the bobbin case, loosen the tension on the case. If the threads pull out too easily and have no resistance at all, tighten the bobbin case. You want the threads to come out nice and smoothly.

When you first start to sew, you may hear a clunking noise. This is caused from loosening the tension disc on the bobbin case. The bobbin is fitting into the newly adjusted bobbin case. When the bobbin has settled into place, the noise should stop. If the noise continues, stop sewing and readjust the bobbin and bobbin case.

Winding the bobbin: Often, the bobbin can be wound on the machine. If the threads are too thick to pass through the machine's bobbin winder tension disc, you will need to wind the bobbin by hand. Most yarns and ribbons will require hand winding. Be careful to wind flat and evenly. Only fill the bobbin three-quarters full. The extra room in the bobbin allows for the thicker threads to relax in the case, which helps to prevent a possible bird's nest in the bobbin area.

Speed of sewing: I always sew at half speed while doing bobbin work, and I recommend you do the same. This will allow you to have control of the machine and allows the threads to come out of the bobbin case smoothly.

Supplies

- Decorative threads or ribbons
- Extra bobbin case
- Cotton threads to match color of decorative threads
- Cotton thread in a contrasting color that has not been used on the quilt
- Schmetz Topstitch 90/14 needle (or similar)
- Free-motion foot
- Open-toe foot

Note: Since the project is layered with muslin, batting, and top fabric, an additional stabilizer is not needed—the quilt sandwich itself will act as a stabilizer.

Marking the Design Area

1. First you need to mark the design area. Place a thread matching the color of the decorative threads you will be using on top and a thread color that is not used on the quilt in the bobbin. In regular sewing or in free-motion sewing, stitch and mark the design guidelines. Remember, you are marking the wrong side of the fabric with the contrasting thread, so your marking will not show on the right side.

2. Prepare the bobbin and bobbin case for the thicker threads. Adjust the tension of the bobbin case as needed to allow the threads to come out smoothly.

This design area has been marked with a contrasting orange.

Marking the area is very helpful for exact placement and coverage. For example, you will likely want to mark around petals and on the edges of any overlays.

Bobbin Work in Free Motion

1. Attach a free-motion foot and drop the feed dogs on the machine.

2. Follow the steps in Marking the Design Area.

3. Place the quilt upside down and sew within the marked area. A suggested stitch is a zigzag stitch (width 2.0, length 0.0).

Try sewing side to side with short and random length stitches. Sew very close for a tighter fill, or very open for an airier look.

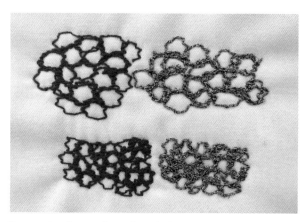

Try sewing in random-size circles.

Bobbin Work with Decorative Stitches

1. Follow the steps in Marking the Design Area.

2. Attach an open-toe foot.

3. Select a decorative stitch. It is best to choose a simple and open design. If the design is detailed and the stitches are very close, this can cause puckering and distortion on the fabric.

4. Place the quilt upside down and sew within the marked area.

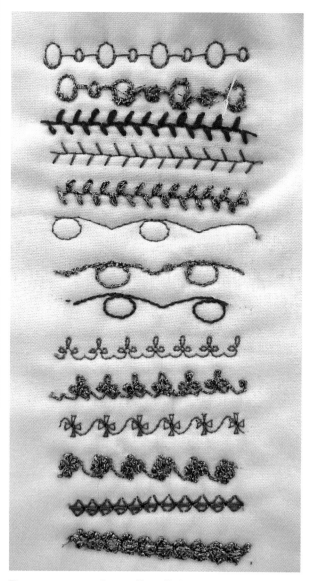

There are many decorative stitches to choose from.

Ideas for Using Bobbin Work

Play and experiment with different threads and stitching combinations. Some threads can have a totally different look and effect with different stitches. Have fun with it!

Trees: Use a zigzag stitch, sewing side to side. Use open stitches for an airier fill. This creates depth where you still see some of the fabric in the background.

Snow and overlays: Use a zigzag stitch, sewing side to side. Sew on the marking lines to cover the edges of the overlays and tree branches.

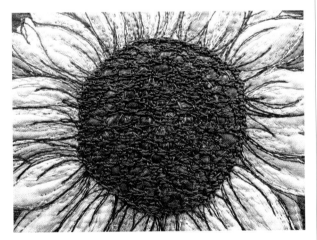

Flower centers: Use a zigzag stitch, sewing in circles. This stitching creates nice fills without using a lot of thread to get a good coverage of the area.

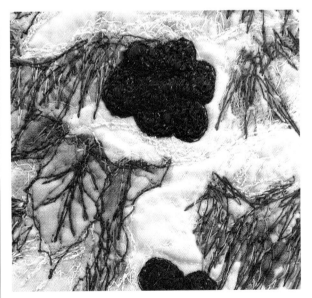

Berries: Use a zigzag stitch, sewing in small circles to get a solid fill of the area.

Speckled berries: Use a different color thread on top than the bobbin work thread. For example, here the top thread is red and the bobbin work thread is yellow.

Thicker lines: Use bobbin work when a thicker line is needed for definition, such as in the bark of this branch.

Decorative stitches: These work great to fill an area with a repeated, exact fill.

Couching

Another way of adding decorative threads, yarns, and ribbons is couching over them with machine stitching. Couching will add texture to the quilt, as the decorative threads/fibers remain raised on the surface of the quilt. A couching foot holds and glides the decorative threads/fibers as machine stitches are sewn over top of them, securing the decoration in place. Couching can be done with free-motion and/or regular machine stitching.

A variety of securing stitches can be used, such as a zigzag or a decorative stitch pattern. The securing threads will show on the top of the couched element. I like to use threads that will match in color so the two elements are not competing with each other. Matching colors has a more natural effect on the quilt, especially on a landscape project.

Couching is effective in all the same ways that you might use bobbin work, but threads are sewn on the top and from the right side of the quilt.

You will need a special couching/braiding foot.

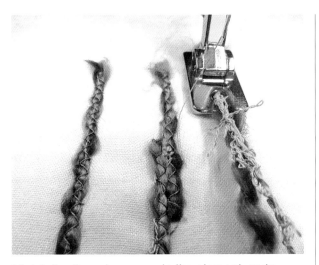

Match the threads you use to the element you're couching to avoid visual competition.

Try couching a vivid green yarn.

Fringe Work

When all thread painting, overlay, and bobbin work is completed and the project still needs additional interest, try adding some fringe. Fringe is a raised three-dimensional stitch that is formed using a fringe foot, also known as a tailor tack foot. The foot has a raised central bar that allows you to only use a zigzag stitch. The bar creates a wider, raised stitch, allowing the thread to rest on the bar between stiches and form loops.

Try couching a glimmering ribbon.

You will need a special fringe foot.

Supplies

- Fringe foot
- Liquid adhesive/fusible stabilizer (if cutting the fringe)

1. Drop the feed dogs and attach the fringe foot.

2. Set the machine for zigzag stitch. Prior to sewing on your project, do a few stitches by hand on scrap fabric to make sure the needle is clearing the bar. You can test the swing of the zigzag stitch and adjust the width if needed.

3. Using free-motion stitching, sew in the same place several times to create a ball-like cluster.

4. When the ball is formed, pull the quilt away from the cluster and form another cluster very close to the first, but in a different direction. This will create an effect that looks like the center of a flower.

Tips and Ideas

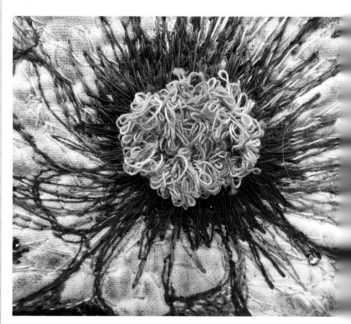

To make flower centers, fill in the centers as densely as desired. Variegated threads work great to create natural shading.

Try using two different-colored threads on the top and in the bobbin. Increase the tension to pull the bobbin thread to the top, creating another interesting effect.

Cut the fringe through the center to create hairlike spikes. Once the stitches are cut, the stitches on the back need to be secured with liquid adhesive or fusible stabilizer. This looks great for hair, grass, shrubs, and the like.

Embellishments

You can never have too many embellishments. Embellishments are the finishing touch, the added step that pulls the quilt together. Embellishments can both personalize and serve a purpose, such as filling in a bare space, correcting a not-straight-enough line, or covering a mistake. Embellishments can be crystals, beads, buttons, yarn, ribbons, raffia, lace, trims, or even a bird's nest. Pull out your embellishments and play until you find the perfect finishing touch.

Crystals

I love when the sun hits crystals and the sparkle draws you into the quilt. A few crystals can change the effect of the whole quilt for the better, but don't add too many—you don't want the quilt to look tacky. Keep the theme in mind; some quilts, such as holiday quilts, can have more crystals without looking too gaudy.

The rows of crystals in this Christmas tree give the effect of strings of lights or garlands.

A crystal at the end of each ray of sunshine lends light to this sun motif.

The crystals incorporated here match the fabric where they are placed, adding just a subtle touch of shine.

Always make sure the glue is fabric-safe when purchasing hot fix crystals. If the crystals are not hot fix, use a heavy-duty fabric adhesive or adhesive such as E6000 glue. To apply hot fix crystals to a quilt:

1. Work in sections of approximately 6" (15cm) square.
2. Place crystals where desired.
3. Place a pressing cloth over the crystals, taking care not to move them.
4. Place the iron on the pressing cloth and heat for about ten seconds. Reapply heat if the glue has not fully melted.

Mixed Fibers

Mixed fibers work wonderfully as filler for areas that look empty or as a blender to soften an area. Fibers can include yarn, silk flowers and leaves, raffia, and more. You can attach them with E6000 or a similar glue or sew them to the quilt. Blend different fibers together to create a natural look. For example, try raffia and mixed threads, or silk leaves and trims.

Raffia is a perfect texture to add to a charming scarecrow.

These fibers add a wild three-dimensional plant touch to a green stitched area.

Buttons

Buttons can be used for many different effects. They can add dimension, provide a pop of contrast, and are perfect to serve as eyes. Use buttons from your own clothes for a personal touch, or find special ones such as the buttons used on the flag panel shown here.

These ornate buttons suit the patriotic theme.

Buttons not only serve as eyes here, but as a brooch for the scarecrow.

Trims and Ribbons

Trims can add texture and depth to a quilt, but ideally they are added for fun. Don't be afraid to add different colors and textures to pull the whole quilt together. Trims can also work great to help form a straight line when needed. If the lines on a quilt became distorted, cover them with a trim to restraighten the line. Finally, trims are also a good choice for covering stitches that you do not want to see on the quilt, such as the stitching on raw edges.

When lines on the quilt are uneven, either from printing or from distortion from sewing, choose a ribbon or trim that is wide enough to cover the line. Draw or chalk a straight line as a placement guide.

Then either glue or sew your chosen trim in place with matching colored threads.

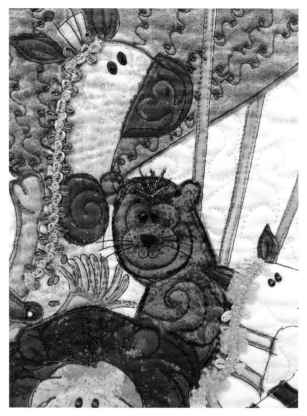

These whimsical trims add pizzazz to the giraffe's and horse's manes.

Both trim and ribbon adorn this hot-air balloon.

You would never know there were little mistakes underneath the pieces of trim on this tree!

An imperfect line is easily corrected with a nice, straight piece of trim.

A matching trim not only adds a flourish, but can hide raw edge stitching as well.

Miscellany

Add items that fit the theme of the quilt. Don't be afraid to have fun and think outside the box when adding an embellishment!

Embossed metal acts as ornament toppers.

An entire miniature bird's nest makes a bold statement.

General Tips

Applying embellishments on the quilt is the finishing touch. Pay attention to the fine details of why, when, and how they are applied. Follow these tips.

- When attaching multiple layers of trims, work from the bottommost layer, covering edges and stitches as you layer. On the tree shown below, silver trim first covers the raw edge of the tree, then lace covers the end of the silver trim, and finally a rhinestone chain covers the stitching that attaches the lace.
- When attaching items where the edges cannot be hidden, finish the edges with a satin stitch or zigzag stitch to prevent fraying.
- When attaching raised items, such as pearls or a rhinestone chain, attach with a beading foot. This foot allows the items to rest in a channel while you sew.

Three different trims have been layered on this tree.

- When attaching a chain/string, leave a 1" (2.5cm) tail behind where you really want to start. This allows for an easier start and exact placement. Attach the item with a zigzag stitch. Always check the swing of the zigzag to prevent the needle from hitting the item. On the first pearl/stone, sew several zigzags in place to secure the item. Repeat at the end of the item.
- When attaching mixed fibers, beads, and buttons, glue and/or sew the items in place with matching colored threads.

A beading foot will make attaching a rhinestone chain or similar much easier.

The embellishments blend in nicely here in part because the threads used to attach them do not contrast with the embellishments or the background.

Finishing a Quilt Project

When all the free-motion quilting, thread painting, and other possible embellishment techniques are completed, the quilt may look quite misshapen and wrinkled. To correct this issue and get it ready for finishing, it's time to block and square the quilt.

Blocking

Before beginning, make sure the entire area for ironing is flat and able to get wet from the steam of the iron.

1. On the back side, iron the quilt with a very hot steam iron from the center of the quilt out to each side. Then iron from the center to the top, ironing up and out to the corners. Repeat on the bottom of the quilt, ironing from the center down and out to the corners.

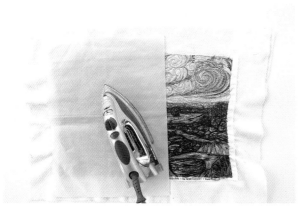

2. Flip the quilt over to the front and repeat the above steps for ironing. Pay extra attention to design elements that need to be straight, such as trees, buildings, and water. Make sure they are as straight as possible. If they are misshapen, pull and tug on the fabric to correct the shape. If needed, use a ruler to check the straightness of the lines.

3. You may need to place something heavy on the quilt, such as books or cans, to help keep the quilt straight while drying. Let the quilt dry completely without moving it. This allows all the fibers and threads to shrink and bond together evenly prior to squaring the quilt.

Remember, if there is an overlay or other potentially sensitive item on the quilt, use a pressing cloth while ironing the front.

Squaring

Once the quilt is totally dry, the quilt can be squared and prepared for finishing.

1. Place your largest ruler or rulers on the quilt and work off of as many horizontal and vertical lines on the quilt as possible (trees, flower stems, buildings, people, water, etc.). Use these reference lines to aide in squaring the quilt.

2. Mark the squaring guides and connect lines on the sides, top, and bottom. Make sure that all batting will be covered when borders or binding is added. Notice how distorted the quilt became from all the stitching.

3. From the marked lines, measure the width and length of the quilt in several places to check to make sure the measurements are all the same.

4. Do not trim the quilt! Proceed to the finishing steps described on the following pages.

After squaring, you need to decide how you are going to finish your quilt. Do you want to frame it, add a border or two, or simply bind it? How about making it into a bag or pillow? The finishing options are endless. We won't get into detail about turning your quilt into something else in this book—there are plenty of great books out there to teach you this—but we'll go over the basics here so you can finish your art panel in a few ways.

Framing a Quilt

This is so easy and adds a professional finish to any art quilt. It's a quick and simple way to finish a project.

1. Block and square the piece.

2. Using the measurements of the squared quilt, have a mat cut to size.

3. Trim the quilt to fit within the size of the frame.

4. Apply E6000 glue or similar to the inner edges of the mat (on the wrong side) and carefully place the mat on the quilt using the marked lines.

> *If you want to use glass on the frame and have added embellishments to your quilt, you may need a shadow box due to the raised surface of the embellishments.*

A finished, matted art quilt.

Adding a Border

If you don't simply want to put a frame around your piece—such as when you want the piece to hang freely on a wall—you will want to either bind the edges or add a border and bind. This is where having the extra batting and muslin that you didn't trim away can work to your advantage. You will sew the borders onto the squaring marks, and the quilt will have an even feel throughout the borders and quilt. There will be no need to butt up or attach additional batting and muslin to the quilt.

Note: If you are not adding any border, proceed to Making a Sleeve and Label and Attaching Backing (page 64).

The instructions below include the measurements given to complete the sample shown. Adjust the measurements for your desired size of borders and finished quilt.

1. Decide how wide the border will be and add 1" (2.5cm). Cut four strips of this width. For the sample, the desired border is 2" (5cm), so the border material is cut to 3" (7.6cm).

2. Place the top and bottom strips on the inside of the square line; this is the placement line. Sew a ¼" (0.5cm) line to attach the top and bottom borders.

3. Flip the top and bottom borders to the right side and press flat.

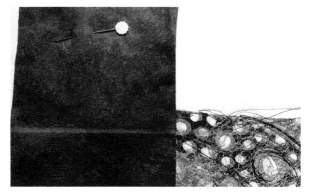

4. Extend the side placement lines onto the top and bottom sewn borders.

5. Place the side borders on the inside of the placement line. Sew a ¼" (0.5cm) line to attach them.

6. Flip the side borders over to right side and press flat.

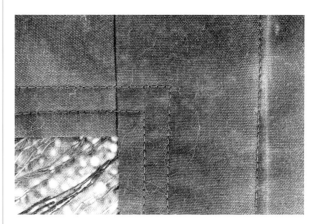

7. Top stitch around the border or quilt as desired. In the sample shown, the border has been double-stitched. Now, if you want to extend the design onto the border, refer to Extending a Design onto the Border, page 64, before proceeding with step 8.

8. Measure and mark a new square line to the desired size of the border.

9. Sew a line ⅛" (0.3cm) inside the marked line to secure the borders. Make sure the borders are laying flat on the batting.

10. Trim the extra border material, batting, and muslin on the marked line.

Extending a Design onto the Border

1. Follow steps 1–7 from Adding a Border, page 63.

2. Apply fusible web to designs from a second panel or coordinating fabric. Arrange as desired, extending into the border.

3. Thread paint as previously done on the panel.

4. Continue with step 8 on page 63.

Making a Sleeve and Label and Attaching Backing

The following instructions are for attaching a clean backing. They include the measurements to complete the sample shown. Adjust the measurements for your piece. If you want to see all your stitching on the back of the piece, skip these steps and instead proceed to completing the quilt by simply adding a binding.

Before proceeding, measure the quilt. The sample quilt shown here in the instructions is 21" x 15½" (53.3 x 39.4cm).

Making a Sleeve and Label

1. Cut a piece of sleeve material 3" (7.6cm) smaller than the width of the quilt x 9" (22.9cm). The sample is 18" x 9" (45.7 x 22.9cm).

2. On both short sides, fold over twice and sew a small seam.

3. Fold the sleeve in half lengthwise (the sample folds to 17½" x 4½" [44.5 x 11.4cm]) and hand press to find the center.

4. Cut a piece of white material for the label. The sample uses a 3½" x 5" (8.9 x 12.7cm) piece. Personalize your label by hand using a permanent marker, or use embroidery or another technique. Place your label on the top half of the sleeve and attach as desired. The sample has a decorative stitch on three sides.

Attaching Sleeve to Backing and Backing to Quilt

1. To determine the size of the backing fabric needed, add 2" (5cm) to the width and length of the quilt. The sample piece uses a 23" x 17½" (58.4 x 44.5cm) piece of backing.

2. On top of the sleeve and the backing, find the center.

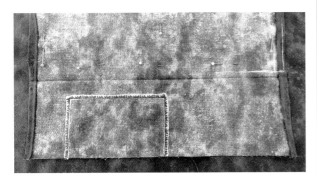

3. Pin the sleeve to the backing along the top edge with right sides together, aligning the centers so that the sleeve is centered. Make sure the label is now on the lower half of the sleeve, or the part not aligned with the top edge at this point.

4. Along the side edges of the sleeve, sew down from the top just until you are ½" (1.5cm) above

the fold mark. On the length of the sleeve, sew ½" (1.5cm) above the fold line. By not sewing to the center fold, an extra space is created for a rod to hang the quilt nicely.

5. Fold the sleeve up to the top of the backing and sew ⅛" (0.3cm) from the top edge to attach the sleeve completely.

6. Find the top center of the backing and the quilt. Pin wrong sides together and sew ⅛" (0.3cm) along the top edge to attach the backing to the quilt.

7. Spray baste the backing to the quilt. Start from the top and work down the quilt in sections.

8. On the front side, sew a ⅛" (0.3cm) seam along the edges of the quilt, attaching the backing to the quilt.

9. Trim the excess backing from the quilt.

10. Thread paint very sparingly on the front of the quilt (add some grasses, curlicues, or outline an item) to secure the backing to the quilt.

11. Attach binding as desired. I use a 2¼" (5.7cm) binding sewn from the front and hand-sewn on the back.

The finished quilt.

Here are three ideas for finishing a quilt.

Double border

Trim used as an inner border

Enveloped finish

CHAPTER 4

PROJECTS

The six projects included in this section cover numerous techniques and creative ideas. I chose these panels as suggestions, not as projects you should necessarily try to recreate stitch-for-stitch yourself. My hope is that you will apply these techniques and ideas to the many new and wonderful panels that are designed every year, choosing panels that speak to you.

Project 1: Euphoria Flower
Techniques used:
- Free-Motion Quilting
- Thread Painting

Project 2: Embellished Tree
Techniques used:
- Free-Motion Quilting
- Thread Painting
- Trapunto
- Embellishments

Project 3: Celebration Flag
Techniques used:
- Free-Motion Quilting
- Thread Painting
- Three-Dimensional Effects
- Embellishments

Project 4: Flowing Dreamscape
Techniques used:
- Free-Motion Quilting
- Thread Painting
- Overlay
- Machine Techniques: Bobbin Work
- Embellishments

Project 5: Snowy Winter Birds
Techniques used:
- Free-Motion Quilting
- Thread Painting
- Trapunto
- Overlay
- Machine Techniques: Bobbin Work
- Embellishments

Project 6: Serene Heron
Techniques used:
- Free-Motion Quilting
- Thread Painting
- Overlay
- Embellishments

EUPHORIA FLOWER

This is a wonderful panel to free-motion quilt and play with threads. This panel is best when you leave lots of fabric showing. Try not to free-motion quilt and thread paint too heavily. Let the fabric and thread work together to create a modern piece of art.

Techniques used

- Free-Motion Quilting
- Thread Painting

Supplies

- 1 panel: Artisan Spirit Euphoria by Northcott (or similar)
- Cotton batting and muslin, 30" x 38" (76.2 x 96.5cm)
- Free-motion foot
- Schmetz Topstitch 80/12 needle (or similar) for background quilting
- Schmetz Topstitch 90/14 needle (or similar) for thread painting

Threads (all Mettler)

Note: for clarity, generic color names are used throughout.

Metrosene

- Tan #1453

Poly Sheen (for bobbin threads)

- Colors to match top threads: green, brown, and orange

Variegated Silk-Finish Cotton 50

- Mixed greens #9818
- Mixed oranges #9858

Silk-Finish Cotton 50

- Rust #1074
- Medium orange #0163
- Dark green #0757
- Medium green #0840
- Dark brown #1002
- Medium brown #0173

Metallic

- Green #5833
- Orange #1134

  Note: Use variegated threads in a zigzag stitch and solid color threads in a straight stitch. Match the bobbin thread colors to the top thread colors.

Original panel

Prepare
Create a quilt sandwich by spray basting the muslin, batting, and panel (see Layering the Project, page 22).

Free-Motion Quilt
Free-motion quilt the background using the 80/12 needle. Use tan thread. Quilt from the top of the panel, moving down to the bottom.

Thread Paint
Thread paint the panel using the 90/14 needle, following the below instructions. For steps 1–2, use a zigzag stitch with a width of 2.0 and a length of 0.0, using variegated threads. For steps 3–11, use a straight stitch and solid color threads, completing several steps within a single design (flower, leaf) at a time for shading, highlighting, and final detail stitching.

Flower:

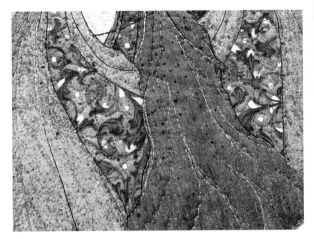

1. Stitch from the left side of the flower, moving to the right. Use variegated orange on the center and side sections of each petal. Do not use on the sections with green in them. For the stitch design, follow the direction on the print. Make lines along the edge of the petal and inside each petal, going from the center and moving out to the edge.

Leaves and leaves in center of flower:

2. Stitch from the top leaves, working down the panel. Use variegated green. Stitch along the center of the leaf, sewing to the edge. Make lines to mimic veins in a leaf.

Flower and butterfly:

3. Use medium orange to free-motion quilt on the orange areas of the petals and butterfly. Try not to quilt onto the green.

4. On the light-colored petals, layer the threads using medium orange, then metallic orange. On the dark-colored petals, layer the threads using rust, then metallic orange. The stitching should blend with the variegated thread. Follow the same flow and direction of stitching. It is fine if the threads overlap—this helps create the shading and blending of colors.

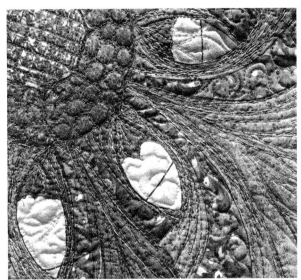

5. Use rust thread on the flower center. On the inner section, sew vertical and horizontal lines, i.e., cross-hatching. On the outer section, sew random size circles. While sewing with rust, also add some detail lines on the bug's body.

Now is a good time to iron the quilt to control distortion and bumps.

Leaves and green areas in flower and butterfly:

6. Highlight the leaves with medium green. Be careful not to add too much thread. Follow the veins created with the variegated thread.

7. With medium green, free-motion quilt the green area of the butterfly.

8. Use metallic green on some leaves to add additional veins and highlights. Also use metallic green on the green sections of the flower petals.

9. Outline and add additional detail on all the leaves and on the green sections of the flower petals with dark green.

Brown threads:

10. Highlight the stems with medium brown.

11. Use dark brown to add highlights and detail outlines on the stems, flower, flower center, butterfly, and bug. This is a good time to assess for bumps in the flower. The bumps can be flattened when adding highlight stitches.

Block, Square, and Finish

Block the quilt. Square the quilt. Finish the quilt as desired. This quilt was finished by wrapping it around a wooden frame. (See Finishing a Quilt Project, page 60, for additional details and instructions.)

EMBELLISHED TREE

Be creative and embellish until your heart is content! This panel works great for trapunto and adding personal embellishments. Add some of your grandmother's laces and pearls to make a one-of-a-kind treasure to keep for a lifetime.

Techniques used

- Free-Motion Quilting
- Thread Painting
- Trapunto
- Embellishments

Supplies

- 1 panel: White Christmas by Northcott (or similar)
- Background fabric, 24" x 36" (61 x 91.4cm)
- Cotton batting and muslin, 30" x 42" (76.2 x 106.7cm)
- ½ yard (0.5m) fusible web (such as HeatnBond Lite), cut into 1" (2.5cm) strips
- ¼ yard (0.3m) lightweight fusible stabilizer (such as Pellon®)
- Liquid adhesive (such as Therm O Web Fabric Fuse)

- Free-motion foot
- Beading foot (optional)
- Schmetz Topstitch 80/12 needle (or similar) for background quilting
- Schmetz Topstitch 90/14 needle (or similar) for tree and adding embellishments
- 3 yards (2.8m) ⅛" (0.3cm) silver ribbon
- 3 yards (2.8m) lace trim
- 3 yards (2.8m) pearl string
- 3 yards (2.8m) rhinestone chain
- Clear crystals in miscellaneous sizes
- Wired ribbons for bows

Threads (all Mettler)

Note: for clarity, generic color names are used throughout.

Background thread
- Color to match new background

Poly Sheen (for bobbin threads)
- Colors to match top threads: dark green and light brown

Metrosene (for top threads)
- Light brown #1120

Silk-Finish Cotton 50 (for top threads)
- Dark green #0757

Metallic
- Silver #0511
- Gold #2108

Note: Match the bobbin thread colors to the top thread colors.

Assemble

1. Create a quilt sandwich by spray basting the muslin, batting, and new background together (see Layering the Project, page 22).

2. On the backside of the panel, iron fusible web strips onto the outer edge of the star, tree branches, and presents. Cut out around the design as desired. The quilt shown was made smaller by removing the bottom branch of the tree.

3. Remove the fusible web backing from the star and top quarter of the tree only. Leave the backing on the remaining part of the appliqué.

4. Center the appliqué piece on the new background.

Embellish

The project is completed in sections. All steps are completed before moving on to the next section of the tree. This helps to keep the tree as straight as possible. You will also be able to get a feel for how many embellishments to add per section.

1. Iron and fuse only the top quarter of the appliqué to the new background.

Original panel

2. Free-motion quilt the background only around the area where the appliqué has been ironed down. Match the thread color to the background fabric. Quilt from the edge of the appliqué to the sides, working up to the star and open areas.

3. With a small zigzag stitch, in free-motion, sew along the raw edges of the star and the tree branches that are ironed down. Use the same thread that was used on the background.

6. Add lace trim on the inside of the tree to form sections of branches. Use silver metallic thread and a zigzag stitch with a width of 1.5 to secure the trim.

4. Within the sewn-down section, complete all steps of trapunto: Outline and sew the area, cut the slit, stuff with filler, then cover the slit with iron-on fusible stabilizer.

5. Cover the raw edge lines on the tree with ⅛" (0.3cm) silver ribbon, then on the star as well. Use silver metallic thread and a zigzag stich with a width of 1.5 to secure the ribbon. Note: Liquid adhesive can be applied to the edge of the appliqué or ribbon to help with accurate placement of the ribbon prior to sewing.

7. Add additional straight stitching on the star, snowflakes, tree branches, and/or balls. Use silver and gold for the star, silver for the snowflakes, dark green for the branches, and silver and gold for the balls.

8. Repeat steps 1–7, working in sections, to gradually move down the tree until stopping before the last branch. Make sure the tree is staying straight prior to ironing and starting the next section. If needed, adjust and straighten out the remaining tree appliqué. If you cut off the bottom branch to make the tree smaller, tuck the presents under the last branch before ironing down.

9. On the last branch, complete steps 1–7 again, but skip step 6—do not add lace trim to the last branch yet.

10. Free-motion quilt the remaining background. Quilt from the sides and move down to the bottom.

11. Thread paint the presents. First quilt with a zigzag stitch (width 2.0, length 0.0) on all raw edges using light brown. Then quilt with a straight stitch with first light brown, then gold, then silver.

12. Sew lace trim onto the last branch.

13. Sew rhinestone chain above all the lace trim and cover the threads that attach the lace. Use a zigzag stitch that is wide enough to clear the rhinestone chain, testing it before proceeding on the project. A beading foot would be very helpful here, if you have one.

14. Add pearl string where desired. If possible, tuck pearl string under the lace trim to hide the ends.

15. Add crystals and wire-edged ribbon bows where desired.

Block, Square, and Finish

Block the quilt. Square the quilt. I used the star as the centering mark, making sure the tree was straight. Verify even measurements on both sides of the bottom branches and presents. Finish the quilt as desired. This quilt was finished with a binding. (See Finishing a Quilt Project, page 60, for additional details and instructions.)

CELEBRATION FLAG

This panel comes to life by adding a three-dimensional effect on the eagle's wings and flag. Add some thread painting on the fireworks and see them exploding as you sew! Finish as a banner in time for Independence Day.

Techniques used

- Free-Motion Quilting
- Thread Painting
- Three-Dimensional Effects
- Embellishments

Supplies

- 2 panels: Stonehenge Celebration 2 by Northcott (or similar)
- Cotton batting and muslin, 48" x 28" (121.9 x 71.1cm)
- ¼ yard (0.3m) lightweight fusible stabilizer (such as Pellon)
- 1 yard (1m) tassel trim
- Free-motion foot
- Schmetz Topstitch 90/14 needle (or similar)

Threads (all Mettler)

Note: for clarity, generic color names are used throughout.

Poly Sheen (for bobbin thread)

- Colors to match top threads: red, blue, white, and brown

Silk-Finish Cotton 50

- Ivory #0778
- White #2000
- Bright red #0504
- Maroon #0918
- Dark blue #0697
- Blue #1305
- Tan #1425
- Dark brown #0264

Variegated Silk-Finish Cotton 50

- Mixed browns #9852

Metallic

- Red #1723
- Silver #0511
- Blue #4101

Note: Use variegated threads in a zigzag stitch and solid color threads in a straight stitch. Match the bobbin thread colors to the top thread colors.

Prepare

Create a quilt sandwich by spray basting the muslin, batting, and panel together (see Layering the Project, page 22).

Embellish

Flag:

1. Free-motion stitch the white and red stripes with matching color threads (ivory and bright red). Quilt in a downward direction, creating a flow in the flag. Finish the red stripes with metallic red.

2. Free-motion quilt the flag's blue background with matching color thread.

Original panel

3. Free-motion stitch the stars with metallic silver.

Flag Holder:

4. Free-motion stitch with metallic silver, followed by tan.

Blue Background:

5. Free-motion quilt the dark blue areas on the background with dark blue. An open design, such as stippling, is recommended. Do not quilt too heavily; additional threads will be used for the fireworks. You are only free-motion quilting here now to stabilize the quilt for heavier thread work later on the fireworks.

Eagle:

6. Free-motion zigzag stitch the eagle with a width of 2.0 and length of 0.0 using variegated brown. Stitch to form feathers, the head, the feet, and the body. This is shown on the left in the photo below.

7. Free-motion straight stitch the eagle using dark brown. Define and outline feathers, the head, the feet, and the body. This is shown on the right in the photo above.

Fireworks:

8. Start with the fireworks on both sides, then move to the bottom fireworks, and finish with the top fireworks. If the fireworks are layered/overlapped, thread paint the fireworks in the background first, then the foreground fireworks. Frequently iron the quilt to prevent possible distortion and wrinkles due to heavy threading on the fireworks. If you plan to trim your quilt to a point, there is no need to quilt all the way to the bottom of the panel.

9. Work with maroon, white, blue, metallic red, metallic blue, and metallic silver. Thread paint, with single lines of stitching, using three different thread combinations on each firework. Layer the threads as desired. For example,

one firework could be metallic red, white, and blue; the next firework could be metallic blue, maroon, and metallic silver. Stitch in the direction or fall of the firework.

10. For a finishing detail, add some additional falling lines in a different color than the last color used. This helps to create the feel that the fireworks are coming out at you.

Block and Square

Block the quilt. Square the quilt, but also include creating a point at the bottom of the panel per the below instructions.

1. Square the top, bottom, and sides to the desired size and mark.

2. On the bottom line, find the center of the quilt and mark.

3. Decide the length of the drop to the point. In this example, the length is 6" (15.2cm).

4. On the sides, measure up 6" (15.2cm) from the point.

5. Draw a line from each side to the center point.

Add 3D Elements

Create and add three-dimensional pieces for the eagle wings and flag (see Three-Dimensional Effects, page 46).

1. Make three-dimensional eagle wings and a flag using a second panel.

2. Arrange the wings and flag on top of the panel to determine placement.

3. Flip up and pin in place, tucking and pleating if needed.

4. Sew very close along the edge to attach the wings and flag.

5. Flip down and tack the wings and flag where desired. Do not sew them down completely—you want to see the lift and dimension.

Finish

Attach the backing and finish (see Finishing a Quilt Project, page 60).

1. Recheck the measurements of the squaring marks. Adjust if needed. Trim the quilt on the squaring marks, including cutting it to a point.

2. Measure the quilt and cut backing that is 3" (7.6cm) longer in length and width. Attach a sleeve to the top of the backing.

3. Center the quilt and backing with right sides together (place the sleeve on the top of the quilt). Pin in place.

4. Sew ¼" (0.5cm) along the edge of quilt to attach the quilt to the backing. Leave a 4" (10.1cm) to 5" (12.7cm) opening on the bottom to turn the quilt inside out.

5. Turn inside out and press.

6. Fold in the seam on the bottom. Topstitch ⅛" (0.3cm) along the edges of the quilt.

7. Attach trim on the bottom of the piece. If the trim has hanging pieces like the tassel trim used, make sure a tassel is hanging from the point. Sew from the center to the right, then sew from the center to the left, keeping the trim centered. Extend the trim around the back for 1" (2.5cm) and sew in place.

8. Add buttons and crystals as desired.

FLOWING DREAMSCAPE

Landscape panels are wonderful; they call for added texture and dimension. The best way to achieve this is by adding some thread painting, overlays, and embellishments. You cannot go wrong; let your creative mind play!

Techniques used

- Free-Motion Quilting
- Thread Painting
- Overlay
- Machine Techniques: Bobbin Work
- Embellishments

Supplies

- 1 panel: Artisan Spirit Dreamscapes by Northcott (or similar)
- Cotton batting and muslin, 27" x 20" (68.6 x 50.8cm)
- Hot fix (Angelina) fibers in mixed sky colors
- Blue glitter tulle overlay
- Pressing cloth
- Free-motion foot
- Beads and hot fix crystals (optional)
- Schmetz Topstitch 90/14 needle (or similar)

Threads (all Mettler)

Note: for clarity, generic color names are used throughout.

Poly Sheen (for bobbin thread)

- Colors to match top threads: blue, green, gray, and brown

Variegated Silk-Finish Cotton 50

- Mixed browns #9852
- Mixed greens #9818
- Mixed blues #9811
- Mixed grays #9861

Silk-Finish Cotton 50

- Light green #0092
- Dark green #0757
- Medium brown #0900
- Dark brown #1002
- White #2000
- Dark gray #1282
- Black #4000
- Sky blue #1464
- Teal blue #1440
- Dark blue #0823

Metallic

- Gold #2108
- Blue #4101
- Green #5833

Note: Use variegated threads in a zigzag stitch and solid color threads in a straight stitch. Match the bobbin thread colors to the top thread colors.

Artisan Spirit DREAMSCAPES • DP21295 • 100% Cotton • by Ira Kennedy • www.irakennedy.com • for NORTHCOTT • www.northcott.com

Original panel

Prepare

Create a quilt sandwich by spray basting the muslin, batting, and panel together (see Layering the Project, page 22).

Overlay

1. Create an overlay sheet with hot fix fibers that is about 20" x 9" (50.8 x 22.9cm).

3. Free-motion quilt the sky area with a straight stitch as desired. I followed the design of the clouds. Start from the center near the tree and move from left to right, working your way up the panel. Do it in layers: start with sky blue, then metallic gold, and finish with dark blue. Be careful to keep the overlay nice and flat while quilting.

2. Place the overlay on the sky area.

Thread Paint

All of the thread painting is done from the top of the tree working down the panel in thirds. Steps 1–7 should be completed in free motion with a zigzag stitch (width 2.0, length 0.0). Steps 8–12 are completed in free motion with a straight stich using solid color threads.

1. Use variegated green on the tree leaves and grass along the sky. For the trees, create circles to fill in the green area. Start from the top and work your way down until filled. For the grass, sew side to side, creating small, varied-length straight lines.

2. Use variegated brown on the tree trunk and branches. Position the fabric so the trunk is horizontal. Sew side to side, creating lines like the bark of a tree. Continue this side-to-side motion to create branches in the tree.

3. Use variegated blue on the top section of the water. Place a blue glitter overlay on the water (only the area that has been sewn) and complete all overlay steps. Sew side to side in the direction of the water flow. Pivot the fabric as needed when the water changes direction. Create ripples in the water. Remember to sew several times over the area that will be trimmed to secure the fibers.

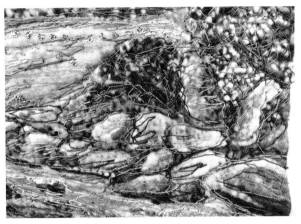

4. Lightly free-motion zigzag stitch the blue field on the left with variegated blue to stabilize the fabric for additional thread painting.

5. Use variegated gray on the rocks in the middle section of the panel. Zigzag stitch larger circles/ovals, the same size of the rocks. Then fill in some detail for shading in the middle. It is best to sew short stitches here, moving back and forth.

6. Use variegated brown on the ground area. Create the same look as the grass, sewing side to side.

7. Continue moving down the panel, repeating the above steps on the remaining bottom third of the panel, working the water and overlay, the grass, and the rocks.

This is a great time to iron the quilt. Remember to use a pressing cloth to protect the overlay. As you move on with additional thread painting, iron the project whenever you see puckering or distortion.

8. Thread paint the tree trunks, branches, and ground area in layers.

- Medium brown, tree trunks and branches: Fill and highlight.

- Medium brown, ground sections: Fill in along the edges to create shading.
- Dark brown, tree trunks and branches: Add more detail inside the trunks. Then outline the tree trucks and branches.
- Dark brown, ground: Add more shading, then outline along the edges.

9. Thread paint the side trees and grass in the middle section in layers. Leave the large tree for last. On each tree, alternate the layering of thread combinations. For example, one tree can be thread painted with light green and dark green, a different tree with metallic green and dark green, and a third tree with light green, metallic green, and dark green.

- Light green, trees: Mimic the circles created with the variegated thread. It's fine to cross over the stitches; this layering is to create depth.
- Light green, grass areas: Fill in shading and highlights along the edge of the water.
- Metallic green: Use wherever added sparkle is desired on trees and grass. Use the same stitching as above.
- Dark green, trees: Add to all side trees. Mimic the same circles as above. It's fine to overlap the prior stiches.

- Dark green, grass: Add additional highlighting and blending. Outline along the water's edge to help create a horizontal line. Randomly add grass spikes in the grass field and along the tree trunks. This will blend and soften the edges along the grass and tree trunks.

10. Thread paint the water in the middle section in layers.

- Sky blue: Add highlighting and shading along the edges of the water and overlay. This is a good time to secure the overlay where it is not well attached.
- Sky blue: Create areas inside of the water to resemble ripples and depth.
- Metallic blue: Add additional sparkle where desired to create shimmering in the water.
- Dark blue: Add additional highlights where desired.
- White: Add along the edge of the water and where the water is falling to create an effect of splashing.

11. Thread paint the rocks in the middle section in layers.

- Dark gray: Add highlighting and shading within each rock. Mimic the grain or detail on the panel.
- Black: Add additional shading and outline each rock. Create a nice line between the rocks and the water.

12. Thread paint the flowers in the field on the left side in layers and in rows. Complete all steps in one row of flowers before moving down to the next row. Occasionally add dark green grass spikes to soften the flower field and make it look more natural.

- Teal blue: Sew multiple spikes together (like grass spikes). Sew these in one row.

- Metallic blue: Use on various flower spikes. This helps to prevent all the flowers from looking the same.
- Dark blue: Repeat the same stitching as done with teal blue.

13. Continue moving down the panel. Repeat the same layering of thread for each element, in order: the grass on the edge of the rocks on the left side of the panel, the large rocks on the left side, the remaining water, the large rock in the center bottom, and the grass in the lower right corner.

Add Final Embellishments

1. Finish the large tree as desired. This quilt was thread painted using the same steps as the smaller trees, and also includes bobbin work stitched in small, irregular length lines to create a nice, natural fill.

2. Add additional embellishments as desired. This quilt had beads and mixed fibers added near rock and grasses.

Block, Square, and Finish

Block the quilt. Square the quilt. I used the horizontal lines of the water and grass as reference lines for squaring. Make sure the large tree bark is straight. Finish the quilt as desired. This quilt was matted and framed. I also made it into a bag! (See Finishing a Quilt Project, page 60, for additional details and instructions.)

I made this panel into a charming tote bag.

Opposite page: Turn the book so you can take in all the gorgeous detail of this finished piece.

SNOWY WINTER BIRDS

This beautiful project incorporates many techniques. Combine two panels to design your own project. Add some thread painting, trapunto, overlays, and machine-stitched bobbin work.

Techniques used

- Free-Motion Quilting
- Thread Painting
- Trapunto
- Overlay
- Machine Techniques: Bobbin Work
- Embellishments

Supplies

- 2 panels: Winter Birds by Northcott (or similar)
- Cotton batting and muslin, 36" x 44" (91.4 x 111.8cm)
- Background fabric, 20" x 50" (50.8 x 127cm) (be aware of direction of cloud placement)
- 1 yard (1m) fusible web (such as HeatnBond Lite)
- ½ yard (0.5m) sheer white overlay for snow
- ½ yard (0.5m) sheer light blue overlay for snow
- 9" x 20" (22.9 x 50.8cm) gold overlay
- Pressing cloth
- Polyfill stuffing
- ½ yard (0.5m) lightweight fusible stabilizer (such as Pellon)
- Free-motion foot
- Schmetz Topstitch 80/12 needle (or similar) for free-motion quilting
- Schmetz Topstitch 90/14 needle (or similar) for thread painting

Threads (all Mettler unless otherwise noted)

Note: for clarity, generic color names are used throughout.

Poly Sheen (for bobbin threads)
- Colors to match top threads: white, dark green, medium brown, and red

Metrosene
- Blue (match color of background)

Variegated Silk-Finish Cotton 50
- Mixed greens #9818
- Mixed light greens #9821
- Mixed browns #9852
- Mixed tans #9855

Silk-Finish Cotton 50
- Medium green #1099
- Dark green #0757
- Tan #1130
- Dark brown #0264
- Maroon #0918
- White #2000
- Dark gray #0348

Metallic
- Silver #2701
- Gold #2108

YLI Candlelight brand threads (for bobbin work)
- Rainbow #RNB (for snow)
- Red #003 (for berries)

Note: Use variegated threads in a zigzag stitch and solid color threads in a straight stitch. Match the bobbin thread colors to the top thread colors.

Assemble

1. Spray baste the muslin and batting together.

2. Spray baste the background to the batting with the background on the left half.

3. On one panel, iron 1" (2.5cm) strips of fusible web to the left edge of the main design.

4. Cut along the left edge of the design as desired.

5. Remove the backing of the fusible web and place the cut panel onto the batting. Extend the design to cover the edge of the background, and iron in place.

Original panel

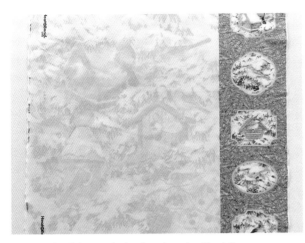

6. Iron fusible web to the top half of the second panel.

7. Fussy cut elements from the panel (such as birds, branches, and birdhouses).

8. Add elements to the left side of the fused panel to create a new design. When you are happy with the layout, iron it in place.

Stitch

This project is completed in sections of three. All steps are completed before moving down to the next section. Work steps 1–5 on the top section before moving on to the middle and bottom sections.

1. Free-motion quilt the top third of the sky with a Metrosene thread, matching the thread color to background fabric. Start from the center top and sew from the center to the left.

2. In a free-motion zigzag stitch, sew the tree branches, working from the left side to the right. Create branch shapes, adding side needles over the green areas on the panels. Use two different variegated greens, alternating the threads and sewing in clusters on the branches.

Blend the branches into each other to achieve a natural look. Also extend the branches into the background.

3. The snow is made with a white and blue overlay. Alternate the different colored overlays throughout the snow areas. This is a good way to cover the raw edges. In a free-motion zigzag stitch, use white thread to attach the overlay on snow areas. Trim away excess overlay.

4. There are two different shades of birdhouses. For the medium brown birdhouses, use variegated brown in free-motion zigzag to create wood grain effects and shading. For the light birdhouses, use variegated tan in free-motion zigzag to create wood grain effects and shading.

5. Outline each bird with a straight stitch in the following colors: female cardinal in tan and maroon, male cardinal in maroon, and all other birds in dark gray.

Iron the quilt flat prior to moving to the next section. Remember to use a pressing cloth on the overlay!

6. When the top section is completed, repeat the above steps on the second section. Remember to free-motion quilt the background before thread painting!

8. For the snow on the branches and birdhouse roofs, thread paint in a straight stitch with metallic silver or do bobbin work with a thick iridescent rainbow thread. Add more detail on the snow. Cover the edges of the overlay, creating a nice finish. It is fine to cover the branches.

7. On the bottom third section, repeat all the above steps again, with the addition of stitching the long bird feeder as follows. Place gold overlay on the feeder, covering the feeder and birds. Sew with a zigzag stitch using metallic gold to outline the feeder and the birds (left). Trim away excess fabric on the sides of the feeder and away from the birds to expose them. Then, straight stitch with metallic gold on the sides and inside of the feeder for detail and to quilt down the gold overlay. For the birds on the feeder, straight stitch around them with dark gray as you did with the other birds (right).

Now is a good time to iron the quilt prior to adding additional techniques.

9. Thread paint the branches in a straight stitch. Use medium green randomly on branches and sew lines to look like needles on the tree branches. Do not use this color thread on every branch. It is fine to add on top of both variegated threads. Then thread paint in a straight stitch using dark green on every branch. Overlap the existing stitching.

10. For the medium brown birdhouses, thread paint in a straight stitch using dark brown. Outline the houses and add additional detail and shading. For the light brown birdhouses, thread paint in a straight stitch using tan. Outline the houses and add additional detail and shading.

12. Outline the berries in maroon, then sew over them several times to get a thick line, or do bobbin work with a thick red thread.

Block, Square, and Finish

Block the quilt. Square the quilt. I used the lines on the bird feeder and houses as references. Finish the quilt as desired. This project was bound with two different pieces of fabric—I matched the binding to the background and the tree, which gives a floating appearance to the quilt (see the photo below). (See Finishing a Quilt Project, page 60, for additional details and instructions.)

11. The birds will be embellished with trapunto. Cut a small slit through the muslin on the back of the quilt and stuff it with polyfill stuffing. Cover the slit with fusible stabilizer and iron in place. On the front of the birds, outline the birds again with a straight stitch and also add some details, such as wings, feathers, and eyes.

The binding for this project was done with two different pieces of fabric so that the binding could match the quilt design very closely.

SERENE HERON

This fun panel lends itself to creating extra depth and texture. Combining two panels, layering multiply overlays, and extending the design onto the border creates extra elements of interest and play with the background and foreground.

Techniques used

- Free-Motion Quilting
- Thread Painting
- Overlay
- Embellishments

Supplies

- 2 panels: Water Garden by Northcott (or similar)
- Cotton batting and muslin, 34" x 48" (86.4 x 122cm)
- ⅛ yard (0.5m) dark blue tulle overlay for water
- ⅛ yard (0.2m) dark blue organza overlay for bird shadow
- ⅛ yard (0.2m) medium blue organza overlay for bird shadow
- Hot fix (Angelina) fibers in Aurora, Watermelon, Cobalt Sparkle, and Calypso Blue
- Pressing cloth
- Free-motion foot
- Hot fix crystals (optional)
- Schmetz Topstitch 80/12 needle (or similar) for free-motion quilting
- Schmetz Topstitch 90/14 needle (or similar) for thread painting

Threads (all Mettler)

Note: for clarity, generic color names are used throughout.

Poly Sheen (for bobbin thread)

- Colors to match top threads: dark blue, dark green, pink, black, and white

Variegated Silk-Finish Cotton 50

- Mixed light greens #9817
- Mixed greens #9818
- Mixed blues #9812
- Mixed dark blues #9813
- Mixed pinks #9847

Variegated Poly Sheen

- Mixed grass greens #9932
- Mixed grays #9920

Silk-Finish Cotton 50

- Dark green #0757
- Medium green #0224
- Medium blue #1078
- Dark blue #0823
- Medium pink #1402
- Red pink #1391
- Dark pink #1421
- Orange #0122
- White #3000
- Dark gray #0348
- Black #4000

Note: Use variegated threads in a zigzag stitch and solid color threads in a straight stitch. Match the bobbin thread colors to the top thread colors.

Original panel

Prepare

Create a quilt sandwich by spray basting the muslin, batting, and panel together (see Layering the Project, page 22).

Overlay

1. Create an overlay with hot fix fibers that is about 20" x 28" (50.8 x 71.1cm).

2. Draw a line with chalk to divide the sky and the water.

3. Place the overlay on the line and cover the clouds in the sky area. Do not cover the dark blue area in the upper right corner.

4. Free-motion quilt in a straight stitch as desired; I followed the design of the clouds. Start from the center, near the heron's legs, and move up and to the sides while working your way up the panel. Quilt in layers, starting with medium blue. Layer with orange, then medium pink, and finish with dark blue to define the clouds and swirls in the sky. Be careful to keep the overlay nice and flat while quilting.

5. Trim away the overlay from the heron.

Thread Paint

Steps 1–10 are completed in free motion with a zigzag stitch (width 2.0, length 0.0). Steps 11–16 are completed in free motion with a straight stich using solid color threads.

1. Position the fabric so the heron is horizontal. Sew side to side with variegated gray on the heron to create mixed length "feather" lines to fill in the area. Start from the head, working your way down the neck, wing, and body to the legs.

2. On the grass on the right side of the panel and above the water line, alternate with the two darkest variegated greens. Sew side to side to create grass spikes/blades.

3. For the water, use multiple variegated blues. Position the panel so the water is horizontal. Start from the water line and work your way down the panel to approximately 2" (5cm) below the heron's head, creating ripples/wavelike lines.

4. Use dark variegated blues for the bird shadow. Sew in the same direction as in the previous step.

5. Add small sections of multiple blue organza overlay pieces where the heron shadows fall on the panel. Attach them using variegated dark blue in a zigzag stitch. Trim away excess overlay. Be careful not to cut the threads.

6. Place a blue tulle overlay slightly above the marked water line that is long enough to cover about 6"–8" (15.2–20.3cm) below the line, including the heron shadow. Attach using variegated dark blue in a zigzag stitch. Trim away excess tulle above the water line and around the water lily pads and grass.

7. Continue the same stitching on the grass blades on the right side as done on the grass in step 2.

8. On the water lily pads, alternate with variegated greens and light greens. Stitch side to side, creating an outline and vein details on the leaves.

9. For the remaining water, stitch as done in step 3.

10. Use variegated pink to stitch the lily flowers. Sew side to side, pivoting the panel as needed to create petals.

This is a great time to iron the quilt. Remember to use a pressing cloth to protect the overlays. As you move on with additional thread painting, iron the project whenever you see puckering or distortion.

11. It's time to complete the heron. Use white, dark gray, orange, and black threads, layering the threads from lightest to darkest per the below instructions.

- White: On lighter areas of the feathers, shade in small, uneven-length stitches. Create featherlike stitches on the neck, wings, and body.
- Dark gray: Blend into the white feather stitches, shading into the darker areas and defining the chest, wings, and legs.
- Orange: On the beak, add threads in the direction of the beak.
- Black: Blend black into the gray feather stitches. Sew the outline of the face, chest, body, wings, and legs. Define the head plume, the top of the wing, and the legs.

12. Use medium green and dark green on the grass on the right side. First add medium green to random leaves. Create a highlight and added detail on the sides of the blades. Then add dark green on all the grass blades to define and add extra shading.

13. Complete the water using dark blue, orange, and pink. Add additional shading with all three colors throughout the water areas. This helps to tack down the overlays.

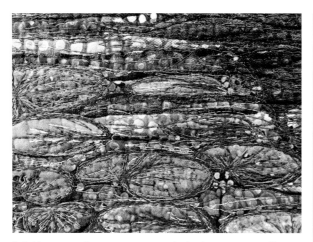

14. Use medium green and dark green on the lily pads. First add medium green to random pads. Create a highlight and added detail on the sides of the pads. Then add dark green on all the pads to define and add extra shading.

15. Finally, use medium pink, red pink, orange, and dark pink on the flowers. For the centers of the flowers, create shading and highlights with alternating colors using medium pink, red pink, and orange on random flowers. Then use dark pink on all the flowers to outline the petals and add additional shading.

16. Add hot fix crystals as desired to the flower centers.

Block, Square, and Finish

Block the quilt. Square the quilt. This quilt was squared off referencing the water line. Finish the quilt as desired. This quilt was finished with the design extended into the border. (See Finishing a Quilt Project, page 60, for additional details and instructions.)

CHAPTER 5

GALLERY

Blue Wreath

Techniques used: Free-Motion Quilting; Thread Painting; Trapunto; Embellishments

Chickadee Wreath

Techniques used: Free-Motion Quilting; Thread Painting; Trapunto; Machine Techniques: Bobbin Work; Embellishments

Eskimo Dance

Techniques used: Free-Motion
Quilting; Thread Painting;
Overlay; Embellishments

Swirling Willow

Techniques used: Free-Motion
Quilting; Thread Painting;
Overlay; Machine Techniques:
Bobbin Work; Embellishments

Original panel

Snowflake Pillow

Techniques used: Free-Motion Quilting; Machine Techniques: Couching; Embellishments

Harvest Pillow

Techniques used: Free-Motion Quilting; Thread Painting; Machine Techniques: Bobbin Work and Fringe Work; Embellishments

Prehistoric

Techniques used: Free-Motion Quilting; Thread Painting; Trapunto; Overlay; Three-Dimensional Effects; Machine Techniques: Bobbin Work and Couching; Embellishments

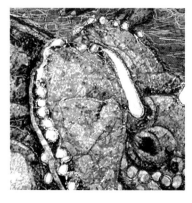

Hot-Air Balloons

Techniques used: Free-Motion Quilting; Thread Painting; Machine Techniques: Couching; Embellishments

Bouquet

Techniques used: Free-Motion Quilting; Thread Painting; Machine Techniques: Bobbin Work and Fringe Work

Poppies

Techniques used: Free-Motion Quilting; Thread Painting; Three-Dimensional Effects; Machine Techniques: Bobbin Work and Fringe Work; Embellishments

Pink Floral

Techniques used: Free-Motion Quilting; Thread Painting; Machine Techniques: Bobbin Work and Fringe Work; Embellishments

Red Star Tree

Techniques used: Free-Motion
Quilting; Thread Painting;
Trapunto; Embellishments

Original panel

Colorful Christmas

Techniques used: Free-Motion Quilting; Thread Painting; Machine Techniques: Bobbin Work; Embellishments

Silent Night

Techniques used: Free-Motion Quilting; Thread Painting; Overlay; Machine Techniques: Bobbin Work; Embellishments

Sleigh Ride

Techniques used: Free-Motion Quilting; Thread Painting; Overlay; Machine Techniques: Bobbin Work; Embellishments

Winter Animals

Techniques used: Free-Motion Quilting; Thread Painting; Trapunto; Overlay; Machine Techniques: Bobbin Work; Embellishments

Witchy Business

Techniques used: Free-Motion Quilting; Thread Painting; Overlay; Machine Techniques: Bobbin Work and Couching; Embellishments

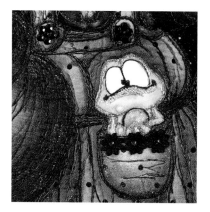

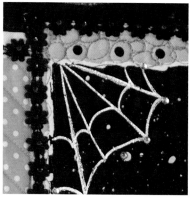

Scarecrow Buddies

Techniques used: Free-Motion Quilting; Thread Painting; Machine Techniques: Bobbin Work, Couching, and Fringe Work; Embellishments

Welcome Friends

Techniques used: Free-Motion Quilting; Thread Painting; Machine Techniques: Bobbin Work and Couching; Embellishments

About the Author

JOYCE HUGHES is an award-winning, self-taught quilter and fiber artist. Her first quilt, made in 2006, was a T-shirt quilt, which she enjoyed making, but she felt limited in her ability to express her artistic capabilities. Within several months, she began to design pictorial landscape quilts using raw edge appliqué, thread painting, and a variety of embellishments. Never knowing the "rules," she broke a lot of them, but with exciting results!

Her first art quilt, "Mother's Day," was entered into the Pennsylvania National Quilt Competition and won a blue ribbon. This has led to numerous awards, recognitions, and opportunities for her in the quilting world.

Joyce loves to free-motion quilt and thread paint. Currently, she is working with fabric panels to create dimension and texture with threads and embellishments, developing a style of her own. Joyce loves to teach and share her tips. One of her greatest accomplishments is when a student in one of her classes creates his or her own artwork following Joyce's dimensional thread painting techniques.

Resources

Amann Group Mettler
www.amann-mettler.com
Threads

Brother
www.brother-usa.com
Sewing machines

Embellishment Village
www.embellishmentvillage.com
Hot fix (Angelina) fibers

Northcott Silk Inc.
www.northcott.net
Fabric panels

Schmetz Needles
www.schmetzneedles.com
Needles

Therm O Web
www.thermoweb.com
HeatnBond and Fabric
Fuse products

Timeless Treasures
www.ttfabrics.com
Fabric panels

The Warm Company
www.warmcompany.com
Batting

YLI
www.ylicorp.com
Threads

Index

Note: Page numbers in *italics* indicate projects.